D0065624

HUNGRY

FOR THE

WORLD

HUNGRY

FOR THE

WORLD

A Memoir

KIM

BARNES

Villard

New York

Copyright © 2000 by Kim Barnes

Library of Congress Cataloging-in-Publication Data

Barnes, Kim.
Hungry for the world / Kim Barnes.
p.   cm.
ISBN 0-375-50228-9
1. Barnes, Kim—Childhood and youth. 2. Women poets, American—
20th century Biography. 3. Barnes, Kim—Homes and haunts—Idaho—
Lewiston. 4. Lewiston (Idaho)—Social life and customs. 5. Young
women—Idaho—Lewiston Biography. 6. Family—Idaho—Lewiston.
I. Title.
PS3552.A6815Z466   2000
811'.54—dc21   99-34851
[B]

Random House website address: www.atrandom.com
Printed in the United States of America on acid-free paper
24689753

Book design by Abby Kagan

FOR BOB —

— WE ARE BLESSED

*We are, I know not how, double in
ourselves, so that what we believe, we
disbelieve, and cannot rid ourselves of what we condemn.*
—Montaigne

When thou hast enough, remember the time of hunger.
—Ecclesiasticus 18:25

HUNGRY

FOR THE

WORLD

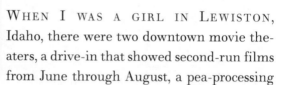 WHEN I WAS A GIRL IN LEWISTON, Idaho, there were two downtown movie theaters, a drive-in that showed second-run films from June through August, a pea-processing plant, and a railroad that ran the perimeter of the town's north side. There were two buildings with elevators to the second floor, and in one sat an elderly man on a chrome-runged stool, his hand on the lever that would take us one flight up and back down. We ate egg salad sandwiches on the mezzanine of Miller's Department Store, where our written receipts were hung by clerks from a wire that turned on its pulleys and carried the paperwork to the accountant upstairs.

Many of the old buildings no longer exist, gutted during a run of summers in the sixties and seventies we all remember as the time of fire, when Main Street seemed destined to burn to the ground, one historic structure after another: the Elks Temple, C.O.D. Laundry, the Hotel Idaho, Kling's, Hughes, The Smoke Shop, but not the store with diamonds and pearls in its windows, whose dividing fire barrier would soon bear a plaque inscribed THE WALL THAT SAVED THE WEST. Had it not been there, the flames might not have been stopped, continuing on to Gibson's Clothing and Aleuridine's

Hall of Cards. A few blocks east, a bar advertising karaoke hides the charred remains of Dave's Drug, where a policeman, responding to an attempted burglary, had thrown himself atop a homemade bomb and saved his partner's life. I can still see the newspaper photo—the single, black shoe left strangely upright, its laces still tied, as though the officer had simply evaporated, let his soul leap up and away.

I remember those mornings thick with the dust of harvest and wind, weeks when the blue sky became something oppressive, not pure but hateful, and the clouds that blossomed atop the Blue Mountains and the Seven Devils at first caught our hope and then our resigned disinterest: not rain but another forest burning, another call for volunteers, another plea for food and supplies. Plumes of smoke rose black and oily from the city's four corners: one day it was the National Guard Armory, torched by an arsonist to protest the slaying of students at Kent State. And then Payless Drug, Shell Oil, Lewiston Tire and Supply. The heat lay in the valley long past midnight, when the old-timers sat on their porches after their garden suppers of tomato-and-cheese sandwiches, cucumbers and Walla Walla Sweets floated in vinegar, late corn made tough by too little water and not enough night. They watched the tugs push their slow way up the Snake, past the confluence and into the narrower current of the Clearwater. They saw how the flat-bottomed barges wallowed heavy with their loads of grain and lumber, and they remembered before the dams and levies, when the rivers had meant something other than commerce, when the bums had claimed the sloughs as their own and slept beneath the cooling leaves of cottonwood.

———

IN THE SPRING OF 1976, when I turned eighteen, there was the whisper of another such summer. The promise was there, in the early bloom of lilacs and dogwoods, in the way people left their windows cracked open at night. My grandmother, Nan, planted her tomatoes early, and she forgot to watch the buds of her cherry trees for signs of late frost. "It'll be a hot one," she said, nodding at the surety of her prediction as she leaned on her rake, scooped a fingernail of dirt from the garden and sniffed it for moisture. Although severely crippled by a childhood illness, she worked her large lot in the cool of the morning and evening, hooking the heavy loops of hoses with her hoe, limping across the yard she meant to keep green. Afternoon was her time of rest. Before her nap, she and I would sit at her dinette, deafened into silence by the swamp cooler's roar, drinking tumbler after tumbler of iced tea, eating the backs and legs of fried chicken. I watched as she snapped the bones and sucked out the marrow—the best for last, she said. I knew, even then, that I would never know such hunger, an appetite birthed by childhood poverty and neglect.

I attended my last week of high school that year in rooms gone still with afternoon sun, my teachers and peers nodding drowsily over their books. There was something in the air, some lull, a husbanding of easy days before the intensity of June and July, the long hours of light.

Vietnam was over, our boys all home, and even in the wake of Watergate, there was room to take a breath, room for the eighteen-year-old males to cast their fate against something other than the draft. The war was a memory now, no danger to us and our dreams, not even mentioned in our class on American history.

Across the top of my binder I had inked the words JESUS SAVES. It distressed me to see the sacred message mocked: the next presidential election was approaching, the first since Nixon's resignation, and placards had sprung up in yards around the city announcing JC SAVES. This stays with me now—the way I viewed the banners and buttons with a kind of horrified fascination, my response tied to the teachings of the Pentecostal Church of God, which pronounced such use of the Savior's name as blasphemy and denounced Jimmy Carter, himself a Southern Baptist, for allowing it. Such sacrilege could bring down the wrath of God upon all our heads and would surely doom the Democrats to defeat.

This was when the world made sense because it had been divided for me into a simple pattern, a perfect plan: on one side, God; on the other side, the Devil. Every man and animal, every celebration and catastrophe, every bloody murder and charitable deed, every bit of food that passed our lips, every drop of liquor that didn't; every fire in every town, every degree of heat and rivulet of water, had been created for one purpose, and that purpose was the glory and magnification of God. What was good in us and the world came from God; that which was evil was allowed by God. Satan had this time on earth to win what souls he could, either through temptation or, as in the case of Job, monstrous injury and pestilence. The Devil could bribe or barter, break us to our knees, but only the failed will of man could allow him a soul.

The fires those years were not simply fires, but periods of testing and purgation. Nixon's betrayal was not simply the act of a power-hungry leader but the manifestation of some deeper rot. Fires and floods, scandal and the failings of men in high places—all were signs of some sin or a need to remember from whom all blessings flow. There was no such thing as luck, good or bad, no such thing as an accidental blaze or an incidental pattern of weather. The rains failed to come for a reason, and the fires began for a reason, and that reason was so that others might come and know the wisdom and worship of God.

Our faith brought with it, as faith will do, a calmness, a patient observation and tallying of signs, for we believed, also, that the Second Coming of Christ was imminent and that fire and drought and evils unleashed forewarned of the Antichrist and the Beast whose number was 666. The Last Days, we called them, and we looked knowingly and with pity on the marchers in Satan's army: the hippies with their long hair and peace signs; the protestors who burned flags and defamed our country—the chosen country, the USA, born of religious freedom and keeper of the Christian flame but fast losing its way.

I had been waiting all my years of awareness for Christ to sound His trumpet and call me to His side. The clouds would gather, then split apart. The earth would shudder, the graves open, and we who were saved would rise, the quick and the dead, in the wink of an eye caught up, made new. But *only* the pure and the holy, those whose sins were forgiven, those who had been born again, whose stains had been washed away by the blood of the Lamb.

So I had been taught, and so I believed until that summer, when, amid the country's bicentennial celebrations, amid the fireworks and politicians' chatter and our preacher's dousing reminders of the fall of Rome, I turned my back on it all: my church, my family, my home, my future made bright by good grades and a nation at peace. I did this for reasons I understood then, reasons that today remain clear: my father's authoritarian discipline; the repressive doctrine of our church; my own stubbornly independent nature. This separation seems as necessary and predictable to me now as did my earlier rebellion, when, at the age of thirteen, I had thrown myself into the world for a trial run. Then, I had been a *juvenile delinquent*, a *runaway*, a minor still watched, protected, and punished by close kin and proper authorities. Not so this time, when I left my father's house as an adult, a young woman still clutching her high school yearbook, on whose pages her classmates had inscribed their names and good wishes.

What path did I believe I might follow outside that door, that gateway into a world from which I'd been protected, isolated, kept hidden? Perhaps even then I knew that the road ahead of me would be a hard one, just as my elders had predicted. Maybe I realized how little desire I had to be sheltered from any of it, for what I desired more than anything were the simple experiences of a life led outside the confinement of dogma and discipline. I wanted all that I had been denied: to go to movies, listen to rock and roll, dance with others my own age and feel the sweet exhaustion of gaiety and abandon. I wanted to be free of the guilt my every need and movement seemed to bring, the threat of my father's censure, the pall of eternal damnation.

I thought I could slide the yoke from my shoulders, like a woman laying down her pails of water. I thought I might brighten and grow stronger with the feel of freedom in my bones, remember again the child I had once been, raised not in the city but in the woods—that sacred place where my father once had lived the life of the lumberjack, where my family had been happy and whole. I did not understand what he had been running from when he left that life, nor did I see how it was that my father was still questing, and that I, his daughter, would continue that quest, unaware of the inheritance I carried with me—the innate need I felt to control my own fate, the very trait that would both scar and save me.

In the heart of a town ticking with fever, I made a decision that would change my life in ways I could not then imagine. Over the next three years I would become a woman I hope never to be again. Yet how can I separate myself from that *other*, that soft girl who hardened in the fire, who came to know of her world far more than any preacher or father had dreamed to warn? She is still with me, and I with her. She is my sybil, my familiar, my reminder of all that I have escaped and come to, who I am when my need is darkest and most true.

Is that child also still with me—that girl who stands beside her mother, leaning against the pew rubbed smooth by chintz dresses and gabardine slacks, raising her hands as her parents raise theirs, praising God in a voice full of first conviction, waiting for the gift of the spirit, the gift of speaking in tongues, the gift that will give to her the language of angels? Is she there in the woods sifting through pine needles for a robin's blue egg, or balancing atop her father's feet as he Texas two-steps her across the floor? I would cling to him in giddy desperation as he waltzed me through the rooms, my head hung back, his arms holding me tight against gravity's dizzying pull.

I want to regain that place I have lost—so much of it now gone, burned by accident or intent. There in the ashes, I might discover some remnant of who I was, some reflection of who I have become, who it is I might yet be.

"NO ONE NEEDS TO KNOW," MY MOTHER once said to me, "what has happened in the past." But without that map, I cannot find my beginnings, trace the progress of my own journey. I must circle back, pick up the threads that bind me to the lives of my parents, in order to understand what brought us to that place in the woods, where our windows had no curtains, our doors no locks, where I did not understand that beneath the nightly narratives of strength and survival that grew and thrived with the telling, there were stories not being told—stories of failure and despair, of chaos and rejection, stories that had been cast off and abandoned like ragged, ill-fitting coats.

At the age of eighteen, my father had left Oklahoma with his widowed mother and his three brothers to come to Idaho. Until the death of his father in a drunken car wreck only months before, their lives had been defined by increasing poverty and the chaos of my grandfather's worsening alcoholism. My father was the second-youngest, the responsible one, strange in his way. In a photo taken in second grade, his hand-me-down overalls hang by one gallus; his hair has not yet darkened to brown. He stares solemnly at the camera with an intensity that is startling, as though it were not the lens he was looking into but the future and the faces he would meet there. Already, he is gauging the world's worth, taking its measure.

As he grew older, my father remained shy but sure of himself. Tall, strong, and handsome, he made his friends and helped his mother, he worked and he hunted, and he read. His brothers and older sister gave him a little more room. He seemed to need it somehow, always going off by himself, preferring his own company, quiet and sometimes brooding. As a teenager, he had his fun. He drank bootleg whiskey, smoked Pall Malls, ran the backroads in whatever coupe his brothers would loan. But from the time he was a young boy, there had been something different about him, as though he hoarded some secret knowledge, some sad awareness, some burden meant only for him to carry.

For my father, his mother, and his siblings, some part of that burden was the tall, redheaded man they each loved with a fierce loyalty. They say my Grandfather Barnes was once a man everyone respected—a good man, quick with his hands and steady on his feet. In the early years no one could grow things the way he could—corn, cotton, hay. When the bordering fields were dry, his were coming up green. Neighbors came from miles around to ask his advice on when to plant, when to plow, what piece of equipment to buy. When injured or ill, they called for him before fetching the doctor.

He could take a beating, they say, then come up swinging. He could work longer, drive himself past endurance. He could drink hard for days on end, then raise himself from his stupor, walk into the field, labor beneath the Oklahoma sun until sweat soaked his clothes and he had rid himself of poison, on into the dusk, the cooling air stiffening the cotton across his back.

What most people feared, my grandfather mastered. In Oklahoma copperheads coil beneath hay rakes, sun themselves between rows of broom corn. The distance a sharp hoe could reach or a shotgun slug could cover was close enough for most. But for my grandfather, the snakes were something he took personally, as though their presence on his small acreage of leased land were a territorial encroachment, some festering of the earth's vindictive nature. He wanted them to feel whatever fear they were capable of, to know that he did not fear them. When he found one in the barn or on the step of the root cellar, or spied one from the seat of his tractor, he would step close, make of his left hand a target, charm the snake into following the flatness of his open palm. With his right hand he would snatch it up by its tail and snap the body like a whip, the head popping loose to roll in the dust, grotesque and skinned down to its small, arrow-shaped skull.

Lucky, brave, gifted with special knowledge. Why, then, did it happen that just as the crop ripened toward harvest, something came to knock it down? Wind, hail, hordes of locust, and only on the farm that he leased and tilled. Everything he put in for the landowner thrived, while a few miles away his own crop died. Not just bad luck, my father insists, but the manifestation of the struggle between my grandfather and God.

My great-grandfather Barnes had been a Baptist minister and believed that this calling had been passed on to his son, a calling that my strong-willed grandfather would not heed. Instead, he began drinking—days when he lived on nothing but alcohol and cigarettes, nights when his own sons would find him at the bar, unable to stand but still fighting, mornings when they carried him from the hidden stills and backroad juke houses, bleeding from falls, beaten and cut by men he fought for moonshine. He was no longer the man gifted with uncommon insight and knowledge but a man who let the whiskey possess him, who allowed himself to forget that he once held dominion over the serpents.

The day my grandfather died—his car slammed into the baked clay of a dry creek bed—my father was miles away on a high school field trip, but he knew: he had dreamed it the night before. Already, he had willed the grief from his mind and taken it from his eyes and buried it deep in his chest. All that was left for him to do was nod when they told him, take his sobbing mother by the hand, and lead her home.

His senior year, he drove the school bus mornings and afternoons and gave his mother the earnings, keeping for himself only enough to buy cigarettes—my father's single and enduring vice. He never forgot the chaos created by his father's failure, how it left my crippled grandmother without comfort or support, engendered his siblings with grief and resentment. That summer he answered his uncle's call for workers in the timberland of Idaho, and it was there that he found the isolation he craved, there where he could labor from sunup to sundown, felling cedar, skidding poles, alone with the noise of the saw and the loader, alone with his thoughts of the way things happened, in his mind a growing sense that he could make an ordered and enduring life for himself, there in that place where the trees grew thick as hair on a dog's back, where a man with a rifle and rod should know no hunger.

It would be not his father's life but a life of his own, and he thought of his sweetheart left behind in Oklahoma and knew that he would call her and she would come and he would have all he might need in the world.

MY MOTHER—FULL LIPS, blue-gray eyes, hair cut short and wisping at her neck and temples—was two years younger than my father, only sixteen the first time he picked her up in his brother's '42 Ford and, with no money for a movie, drove for hours around the Oklahoma backroads for no other reason than to be in her company. They cruised Highway 66, through Arcadia, Wellston, Stroud, Depew, past the oil rigs and hog barns, marginal farms and corner bars. Sometimes they went with friends to the drive-in movie in Oklahoma City, hiding in the car's trunk so they wouldn't have to pay the quarter each, holding hands in the backseat while William Holden and Jennifer Jones pined their way through *Love Is a Many-Splendored Thing.*

Her own family waylaid by wanderlust and alcohol, my mother lived with her grandmother on a dairy ranch. Her father had been a professional gambler in Oklahoma, a con artist, a grifter, never content to stay in one location long enough to let his game catch up with him. Her first years were spent in a constant state of financial and emotional flux: depending on her father's winnings or losses, they were filthy rich or dirt poor. They left town in the dead of night, arrived at the new motel with the sun just breaking the horizon. My mother's self-awareness came to her stained and secreted. Even now she fights her desire to hide.

They went well together, my mother and father, high

school sweethearts, both tall and good-looking, both possessed of the same need to escape, to remake themselves. It was 1956 when my paternal grandfather died, and that year, too, when my mother, at the age of sixteen, joined my father, leaving the red clay fields of broom corn and cotton for a high-elevation camp in the wilderness.

IN THE WOODS, in the logging camps and exhausted boomtowns of northern Idaho, my life was defined by simple existence, or so it seems now. My first home was a wooden trailer, eight feet by twenty, with no water, wood heat, a table, two chairs, and a bed. All around me, the forest rose so high I could not see the surrounding mountains. Except for my extended family and a few itinerant sawyers, we were alone, but I did not know this. What I knew was the early warmth of a tamarack-fueled fire, the whistling of elk calves outside my door. There were venison and huckleberries in the fall, beans and bacon in the winter, brook trout all summer long. There were the creeks full of mussels and minnows, the air buzzing with crickets and locusts, the grass spiced with sage, wild onion, and fennel. Always, there was my mother, never far, warming herself in the sun of late June, preparing our meals, sprinkling the laundry while I read about the engine that could and the saggy baggy elephant and Little Black Sambo who melted the tiger into butter.

My father left for work and came back, his movement sure as the beginning and ending of our day. In the fall he would leave before dawn to find deer and elk, and I would sit at the window and wait for him to come home, back from that place that was full of things dark and wild, full of danger and adventure—where I would have gone, too, if they'd have let me. But I was a girl and too young to go so deep into the forest.

He came out of the woods into the circle of our logging camp, his teeth flashing white, his brown hair thick beneath his cap. He held his rifle in one hand, a yearling buck slung across his shoulders. Blood flowed down his arms—the trail of it led back into the shadowing trees. When I ran to him, he slid the gutted deer to the ground and gathered me up against his chest so that I, too, might feel the strength there. When he sat me down, the print of his hands remained, a brush-stroked swirl of palms, fingers and thumbs.

I followed him to the shed, where he severed the deer's head with a hatchet, hung it by its hind legs, began the skinning—the joint slits, the quick cuts through membrane and tendon. He took the hide in his fists and peeled it down, grunting with the effort. It made a ripping sound, like tape torn from cardboard. He sent me for hot water and vinegar, and I held the heavy bowl as he dipped the rag and wiped the meat clean.

And then to the washhouse, with its wood-fired cookstove for heating water, its wringer washer, its communal shower, where my father rolled his sleeves and scrubbed his arms with soap. The water, tinctured red, ran from his hands into the drain, the pipe, out into the meadow where, in early summer, moose came to graze.

"Come here," my father said. He lifted me to the sink, and I felt the cold sting of water pumped from the spring. He took the towel from its nail and dried my hands between his own. Outside, the air had lost its color. I breathed in the sharp and familiar smell of wood smoke. Across the clearing, I could see that Swede the sawyer had gone to town; his eight-foot wooden trailer looked abandoned without lamp or smoke, and I wondered if he'd be sour when I fetched him for breakfast.

The house of my great-aunt and -uncle sat higher on the hill, supported by a foundation of concrete, more permanent than our base of tongue, hitch, and wheels. They surely had turned in for the night—my aunt with her hair washed and wrapped in tight curlers, my uncle with his whiskers and rough voice—because the next day was their Sabbath and they must drive to town for church.

We stopped, my father and I, so that he might strike a match: for a moment, all the light in the world blazed in the cup of his hands. When the fire went out, I closed my eyes, then opened them to a bank of stars. My father traced the Little Dipper's handle with the red ember of his cigarette, and the outline became something solid, a trail leading toward Polaris—the brightest, my father told me, the one I might always find myself by.

Our trailer made of pine boards was warm, the windows dewy with the steam of my mother's cooking. We stomped our feet, left our boots at the door. I didn't like the brown beans she had prepared, and so I crumbled my cornbread into a bowl and covered it with milk. In the morning, hours before the horizon lightened toward dawn, my father would do the same—it would keep him full while he cut and limbed and skidded the timber from which we took our living.

My brother, Greg, slept in my parents' room, in the crib I'd known as a bed the first four years of my life. But I was five, and I must share. Whenever he gurgled, we stopped our chewing and waited. I thought it was my silence that lulled him back to sleep. I wanted this time with my mother and father to last without interruption. I wanted the snow to come soon, sugaring the windows shut. I wanted one path to the outhouse, one to the woodpile, one to the shed where the deer hung, so that we might stay warm and eat but not have to leave for work or town.

Outside, the wind rose, the darkness rolled in, night bellied up against our windows. Full and sleepy, I lay on the couch and watched my mother wash and rinse the dishes; my father watched too, sitting and smoking, his legs crossed, his socks damp with the sweat of his boots. The coyotes yipped and howled, but I wasn't afraid of what was outside. We were safe, with our light and heat. When I woke, I was in my father's arms, being carried toward bed, the lights going out behind us as my mother followed. My father laid me down and covered me. I curled away from the cold sheets, curled into myself like a leaf touched by fire.

They whispered to each other across the small room—my mother's light voice, the deeper resonance of my father's. I heard the crib rattle, felt the weight of my parents settle on either side of the bed, the warmth of bodies, the cotton long johns they both wore to fend off the chill. They kissed once, twice, in the air above my head, then my mother lay with her back to me so that she might nurse my brother, who murmured and suckled, hiccupped and coughed. I felt my father shift, the solidness of his shoulders, the long length of his spine.

I was warm, the bed gently rocking with the movement of an arm, a leg. I could not fall or be snatched away. Nothing could find me there in the nest they had made for me, and when my mother rolled my brother onto her chest and then over between us, I smelled his sweet-milk face and the musk of her breast. All around I felt the bodies, the close boundaries. My fingers traveled the seam of a thermal sleeve and I slept, and I dreamed of nothing beyond the clearing, beyond the meadow where the elk would whistle their calves in. I did not dream of the deer where it hung from the rafters, turning slowly in the current of wind sifting through barnboard. It was safe there from the bear, who came for garbage, and from the coyotes, who came for bones. When I opened my eyes, I saw nothing but a rivet of star through glass.

I HAD ALL THAT A CHILD COULD NEED and more: loving and devoted parents, a doting grandmother, a tight-knit clan of aunts, uncles, and cousins. Raccoons trailed their kits across the meadow we called our yard. The creeks were full of tadpoles and bullfrogs, brook trout lured to strike by nothing more than a bit of red cloth. We gathered pinecones in burlap sacks and sold them to the Forest Service for pennies a pound, hands sticky with pitch that my mother scrubbed off with turpentine. In August we spent entire afternoons squatting among the huckleberry bushes, wary of bears, buckets hung from our belts, our mouths and fingers stained blue. My mother and aunts made afternoon picnics and sat with us around a large stump of red fir, tablecloth and napkins, peanut-butter-and-jelly sandwiches cut into neat triangles, red Kool-Aid coloring their lips. My uncles, still young and given to play, chased us with towels that snapped and stung; I remember the feeling of ecstatic fear—hysterical exhilaration heightened by the sound of a large man galloping behind me, howling his own soul's delight.

Perhaps we were all children then, my elders barely into their twenties, most of them orphaned and carrying the weight of their own parents' bitterness—a bitterness brought on by weather and grief and a country's depression. Perhaps I am not the only one who remembers those days in the wilderness as full of teasing and laughter, days when the work was hard and the good times easy, when supper came not from the butcher or corner market but from the stream only steps from our door, the ravine behind our circled trailers.

There was no fear, no need to padlock our doors. What out there could hurt us? What worries my parents harbored about foreign missiles and communism and the rising conflict in Vietnam were kept from me. Without newspapers, radio, or TV, we were protected from the turbulence of war and social unrest. My father had found his sanctuary, my mother believed that her happiness lay in his, and I rested between them, secure within the walls they had built for me.

I REMEMBER DAYS OF RAIN when my father took the puzzle from atop the refrigerator and spread it across the oilcloth-covered table. I helped him turn each piece face up, and together we began to create the frame—corners first, then each side connected, blocked in, until the outline was whole. Still, the clouds had no shape; the horizon was a line without direction. It was impossible that all the bits would come together. "But they will," my father assured me. I would see.

Often my father worked on the puzzle for hours, long after I had given up and slid from his lap, weary of so much concentration. Sometimes I stayed and watched him at the table, a single piece in his hand, which he turned and turned on the hub of his finger and thumb. He would remain there beneath the light long after his family had gone to bed, and we would hear the soft click of cardboard, like the *tick-tick* of birds on the tin roof.

When he was finished, he would call me so that I could view the miracle of his work: the table a bloom of red and yellow tulips, behind them the windmill, and behind that, the high, rising mountains capped with snow. "You see," he said. "It just takes patience." But what lay before me had not come from patience, nor even from that far-off land of Holland—it was my father who had made the fields to blossom in wondrous colors; the mountains had grown large beneath his hands.

I wanted to be like him. I wanted to rise each morning before dawn, eat my breakfast of pancakes and bacon, pull on my calked boots at the door, and go into the world that was waiting for me. *Out there* was the life of the lumberjack. *Out there* exciting things happened: the machinery racketed and grumbled, the saws pitched and whined, the trees hit the earth in *whumps* that rattled our windows. *Out there* was where the coyote began its song and the bear snuffled for wild hyacinth, where my father found fawns hidden in Johnsongrass, where nests of baby birds floated down from limbs like wind-sailed bonnets. *Out there* was where the men, called from their skidders and peaveys, fought the summer fires that raged and threatened to consume us whole, where they dug the ditches and set the backfires that saved us. It was then that my father came home mottled with ash, flushed with heat and the war he waged.

But I was *here*, in the small house with my mother and my brother, and though it was a good place with its warmth and closeness, smells of fresh bread and fried venison, it was not *out there*, where the stories came from. The stories were of danger and survival, split-second decisions, moments of courage—the stories my father and uncles told while picking their teeth with broom straw, while the women cleared the plates and sliced the pie and made another pot of coffee. They told of riding the boom to the top of the loader, jumping clear when they heard the snap of a snag knocked loose by sudden wind. They told of the chainsaw kicked back, the deck broken loose, logs rumbling down the hillside and no time to run. They shook their heads and laughed, for this was good fun, having lived and survived so much.

They came home smelling of balsam and diesel, smells I loved. At dinner they smelled of Old Spice and Lucky Strikes and Vitalis, and this, too, I breathed in and savored. There was comfort with my mother and my aunts and grandmother, comfort in their incense of Ivory and Emeraude, yeast and cinnamon. But it was the men I listened to, their strength and freedom that I envied.

I will be like them, I thought. I will go and not stay behind but take up my axe and shoulder my rifle and step out into that world beyond the clearing, beyond the wooden trailers with their narrow windows and heavy doors. They would tell me, all the days of my girl's life, that I wanted too much, that it was not my place, that such thinking would undo me— where did I get such ideas? My imagination, they said, ran wild.

And so I waited, with the other children and women, and I dreamed, and I watched my father leave and come home, and I saw that he was happy. My mother was happiest when he was with us, and I watched her, too. This was her life: she rose to make breakfast; she cleaned, she sewed, she ironed; she baked my father fried pies golden as the moon, oozing apricot filling. Sometimes she called across the clearing to my aunts, and they gathered in the kitchen to drink coffee and smoke and paint their nails. She combed her hair and put on her makeup before my father came home, knowing that a man would not want a woman who let her looks go. She pulled my hair back in a ribbon—she wanted me to look pretty for my father when he returned home. I understood that this was what I must learn: to honor the man's place with the offering of my hands and body. *Here is this face; kiss it. Here is this food; eat.*

THIS IS THAT PLACE that embodies all my child's lost innocence, that piece of myself I left behind, there in the bitterbrush shot through with deer trails, somewhere along the creek banks lined with lupine. It has dropped from my pockets like the lead sinkers that weighted my hooks; it has slipped from my hands like the fish themselves, escaped back into the deepest of waters. It is who I was yet becoming, my feet growing long beneath me, my bones lengthening their stride. It is my mother at the door in her nightgown, my father leaning in to kiss her before disappearing into the early-morning dark, in which he would work until the summer heat shut them down, the danger of fire too great. It is in the river's lost current, the North Fork of the Clearwater before the dam, when the water ran an icy jade, when my brother and I lay on blankets and played in the shallows, ate watermelon and drank iced tea from the canvas-covered water bags dipped in the river to cool. It is in my mother's warmth as she bundled me, wet and shivering, in a towel, my father dozing close by, beneath the drapery of cedar.

I did not yet know who I was, sitting along the banks of the river, on ground that, in less than ten years, would be flooded beneath five hundred feet of water. I did not know that the dam would be built forty miles west at Ahsahka, where the Nez Perce fished the sacred salmon, that there would come a time when the native salmon no longer made their ancestral run for home. What I knew was that everything was as I wanted it to be, and that when I woke from my nap there would be cold pork chops wrapped in wax paper, macaroni salad, and the deviled eggs my Aunt Mary was famous for all across the county.

And so I napped, and even in dreams my curiosity led me, for there was a way that things worked and the secrets were everywhere: inside the periwinkle's lacquered cocoon was a grayish worm that I peeled from its shell and used for bait; if I dug deeply enough, I could find the ground squirrel's burrow, its nest of soft moss and twigs; behind the washhouse was a dump, a treasury of broken crockery and blue bottles, some still holding the dregs of remedy. I could barely wait to begin again—turning the rocks, parting the fern, stirring the water to roust the crawdads flashing orange and red and mottled brown.

In that place of possibility, I did not yet know that there was a battle being waged for my soul, that the man who lay near me, that the woman whose lap I rested in, were searching for safe haven from the evil they believed might swallow us. By the time I was thirteen, I would have forgotten the small pleasures of discovery, my world used up and ugly. By then I would have come to understand that it was Eve who desired the fruit and its store of hidden knowledge, Eve who had damned us all from the Garden. Years away from that child sleeping in her mother's arms, I would enter into my young woman's life knowing these two things: by my gender I was cursed, and my mind would destroy me.

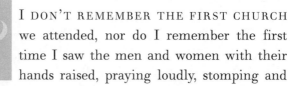 I DON'T REMEMBER THE FIRST CHURCH we attended, nor do I remember the first time I saw the men and women with their hands raised, praying loudly, stomping and clapping, swaying, dancing, some falling, some weeping, some singing a solitary chorus in a sweet, high note. Nor do I remember that moment when I laid my own soul on the altar. I must have been nine, maybe ten—coming into my age of awareness, coming into possession of my own destiny, my own free will.

It was my mother's example I followed: at the urging of the minister who had married her and my father, she had begun attending the Pentecostal Church of God. She missed the friends she had left in Oklahoma, missed even her fractious uncles, her grandmother, whom she had left crying on the porch of the farm. In the church she found women who called her Sister, a family willing to take her in.

It was then that I watched my lovely mother put away her makeup and jewelry, summer shorts and swimsuit, as directed by the dictates of her new faith. As a woman, she must compensate for the flaw of her gender by extreme modesty. Her hair was her glory and could not be shorn. For a woman to don pants mocked the male's superior station. Her arms must be covered, her shoulders, her knees—any part of her that might entice, intrigue, attract, cause another to sin. Silence was her virtue.

It is here that the few stories I have of my mother end—those tales of her youthful courage, how she had sped down the rutted logging roads in her brother-in-law's '47 Chevy, kicking up dust for miles; how she clambered onto the running board of the timber-loaded truck her husband steered down the steep mountains, its brakes lost to roots and stumps, how, at the tightest of corners, she held to the door and side mirror and sailed like a tethered kite above the drop-offs and gullies; how she was not afraid of the bears or the absolute darkness or the height to which a stiff-boomed jammer might take her.

This was before the minister held her beneath the cold water of Orofino Creek and raised her up reborn; before the women of the church had shown her the way with their own plain faces and long skirts, their Bibles whose pages held the teachings of Paul, his warnings concerning the capricious and treacherous female nature; before she bowed her head and covered her shoulders freckled with sun and said, "Teach me to do Thy will."

She had found the order she believed would negate the past she feared might one day manifest itself in her own life: the alcoholism she saw as her birthright, the violence and dislocation. Her silent and submissive role was an extension of the self-protection she had learned while growing up with a father made rageful by his weakness for drink and his frustrated desire for wealth, a man who ridiculed her for every mistake, until her very existence brought with it its own kind of humiliation. Here was a way to redeem her future, a place far away from the rejection and shame. She came home from her meetings glowing, collected, and still.

My father watched her, listened as she spoke of her new-found peace, her absolute salvation. He read the Bible she had left near his chair. Soon after my mother's conversion, he laid his own soul upon the altar.

The Scripture was familiar to my father, but as he began to study more carefully the teachings of Christ and His follow-ers, he came to understand how his own father's life had been ruined by willfulness. How different would it have been had his father heeded his call to the ministry, taken up the cross instead of the bottle, if it had been tent meetings where he met his brethren and not the riotous bars where he badgered the man with the moonshine into floating him another jug?

My father vowed that he would do God's bidding without question, and in this way he would gain salvation not only for himself but for his family as well. He would embrace the faith his own father had abandoned, commit himself to a life of spiritual submission, gain absolution for all past sins.

Here, too, was argument for the simplicity he longed for. He possessed a holy man's antimaterialism; his contentment often seemed linked to our lack of anything beyond the barest of necessities. Even after we had moved from the camps to the small logging towns, when we lived in houses with running water, my father preferred to stop at the spring and dip his hand and drink. Given a choice between an out-house and an indoor toilet, my father chose the rough-hewn privy. He was a loner, a hermit, a would-be anchorite, if not for his family, whom he loved, and his need to support them. But now his eccentricities, his seeming lack of ambition,

were no longer odd or ignoble but necessary to his quest toward spiritual enlightenment.

It seems, too, that my father's inherent mysticism had to
find this home. In the time and place of his childhood—in
the Oklahoma Bible Belt—his uncanny sense of the future,
his dreams that seemed less dream than prophecy, must
needs come from somewhere, and as far as his people knew,
there were only two possibilities: such powers came from
Heaven, or they came from Hell.

After his redemption, my father's dreams were no longer
dreams but *visions:* sometimes they foretold the future,
which he could not change. Sometimes they were apparitions—demons that fouled the air with their breath. There
were times when he fasted and prayed for days so that God's
will might be made clear.

This new father was the same and not the same. He still
played the guitar and sang in his fine tenor's voice, but now
the songs were not the country ballads he'd learned on the
leaning porch in Oklahoma; now they were songs of redemption and revival. Instead of Zane Gray and Louis
L'Amour, he spent his spare moments immersed in the King
James Bible. When he read, we knew not to interrupt him,
not because he might be angry but because it would do us no
good: once fixed on his chosen text, nothing short of a shout
could gain my father's attention, and no one in our house was
allowed to raise his or her voice except in prayer.

The church reinforced our family's already existing patriarchal structure—God to rule over man, man to rule over
woman. The man was the physical and spiritual leader, the
lawgiver, the interpreter, the one on whom the task of discipline fell most heavily. No decision could be made without

his approval. My father's authority had always been absolute, his command of every aspect of my life unquestioned. He believed, as his own father had believed, that a child's love for her parent came only through respect and fear. Stoic and not given to negotiation, my father ruled with the intensity of his eyes and the strength of his hand. Any breach of proscribed conduct was met with immediate punishment, and that punishment was most often a spanking made more agonizing by my being sent to my room to await and think about what I had done. I would lie on my bed wide-eyed, listening for the sound of my father's footsteps coming down the hallway, the slap of the leather belt in his hands.

After his conversion, the discipline my father meted out came just as surely and suddenly as it always had, but now my misbehavior displeased both him and the Heavenly Father, whose punishment, I was promised, would be even greater.

What both my father and my faith demanded of me was complete obedience, the total submission of my will. And it was my will, even at a young age, that I seemed unable to surrender. I learned early on how not to cry when whipped, to let the sting of the hand turn from burn to icy numbness, to let the arm wear itself out trying to draw from me tears. I never learned to give in, make it easier on myself, pretend the chastisement I did not feel. Stubborn, strong-natured, my elders said, and shook their heads in foreboding.

But it was not so simple. Along with unflagging obedience, there was this other, seemingly contradictory thing that my father required: he wanted me to use my mind. It was my father who taught me to question, who teased me with riddles and word games, asked me to tell him which way the wind was blowing, how many miles we'd traveled at certain speeds, why it was that Christ insisted upon washing the feet of Simon Peter even though it was the disciple's heart that bore the greater stain.

From my father I learned to challenge the explication and interpretation of Scripture. He spent hours referencing and cross-referencing various texts. He argued loudly and obstinately with ministers, evangelists, and deacons, taking, I think, his greatest pleasure in the argument itself. Like him, I read from my Bible each day, so that by the time I was in fifth grade, I had memorized any number of begetting lineages, and I knew that *dross* was the imperfection that must be separated from the pure, just as Christ would return to claim His church and leave the sinners behind. It would be years into my adult life before I realized the relative, physical limitations of our holy text: the story of creation and original sin, only a few chapters long, goes on for pages and pages in my mind, so carefully had I been taught to embellish the Garden, the conflict, the Fall.

Reading was my solitude, my escape from boredom, from my younger brother's demands to play, from my cousins and their constant bickering. Even after we moved closer to town, into a frame house with interior walls, we were still miles from the nearest television, isolated by the impenetrable barrier of mountains and trees so that the only radio we pulled in were the midnight skips from a station in Texas. I would read not only the Bible but whatever script came into my hands. The club my mother had joined in my name gave me the miracle of books by mail, and I raced my brother home from the bus on days we thought the thick cardboard envelopes might come. Cereal boxes at breakfast, the instructions on cases of motor oil, the trials of Bazooka Joe—I was ravenous for words, for some connection to the outside world. I read the set of *World Book Encyclopedia* and Children's Classics my parents had purchased when I was in third grade, cover to distant cover. *Robin Hood, Science World, Le Morte d'Arthur, Big Red:* I learned about the universe in which I lived from the pictures and tales, and from the words whose sounds I did not recognize but hoarded like a raven nesting silver. I learned *puma* and *ermine; friar, Excalibur, longbow, Fey Morgan.* I learned that the Eskimos wear boots called *mucklucks,* that Nez Perce ate *pemmican* made from venison and the boiled berries of *kinnikinnick.*

I was teased by peers and berated by uncles for burying my nose between pages. My poor eyesight was blamed on too much reading, as were my allergies and pale skin—all that lingering over the impossible, all those daydreams and big words that put even bigger ideas into my head. But it was my father who encouraged and challenged me. "Look it up," he would say. "Find out for yourself." From him I learned the nuance of language, how each phrase could be read and reread, each time different. Words were jewels to be turned and examined for every facet, every refraction of light. The only absolutes were the legalities of my faith—the rules for behavior and salvation—and my father's authority, his word that could not be questioned.

I wonder now if my father may have foreseen that the analytical skills with which he engendered me might someday lead me away from the beliefs he himself embraced. For even as he insisted that I think for myself, he cautioned me against thinking too much. To think was to know, but the desire to know more than had been granted was blasphemy.

There were doors that must not be opened, passages that must be foregone. Satan lurked there, waiting to snag the wayward traveler, to lure him away with the promise of wisdom, knowledge—the fruit of the tree that Eve could not leave be.

BY THE TIME I was eleven, the easy companionship my father and I once shared was gone. My sudden maturation had caught us both by surprise. I remember one evening near the end of my fifth-grade year, lying back in the tub so that my mother could rinse my hair. The Prell shampoo, stringent as paint remover, got into my eyes, and I let out a howl of pain that reached my father where he sat in the living room, reading his Bible. He thundered down the hall and swung open the door, thinking only of injury. The sight of my unclothed body froze him where he stood, and I saw the look on his face turn from alarm to embarrassment and then to anger. This intimacy was not to exist between us, and I, through my babyish caterwauling, had forced him to see what should remain hidden. For days afterward, I believed it pained him to be near me, so shamed was he by my nakedness.

I was no longer that little girl he'd once led through the dark, my fingers wrapped around his thumb. I was an *early bloomer*, my grandmother said, and I cringed with the words' connotations: images of flowers and creepers and verdant grasses sprouting from the sleeves of my blouse, the waistband of my skirt. I was too aware of my body's sudden transformation, my need for bras and deodorant and feminine hygiene—all "private things," my mother whispered, and I cringed yet again, unable to disassociate the word *private* from the parts of myself that most humiliated me. The chaos of my own body became unbearable, and I welcomed the long skirts and high necklines, the coverings that kept me concealed and contained. My full-immersion baptism in the frigid current of Reed's Creek was a blessing—the water that set my teeth to chattering pure forgiveness, purging me of all sin, washing me clean.

THE WORDS MOST OFTEN USED to describe the religion of my childhood—charismatic, evangelical, Pentecostal— indicate little other than its particular theological concerns. The fact is that we believed in the physical existence of Satan and angels, believed that the skies would break open and God would return to gather His chosen ones home, and that we were those chosen few. We listened to the missionaries tell of dark heathens who practiced the Devil's art, casting spells and bedding witches. They ate the flesh of white babies. They could assume the shape of any man or animal and speak with honeyed voices. We practiced our own small exorcisms, commanding Satan to leave, and I watched those who were afflicted shudder beneath the preacher's hand, watched them fall and writhe, and I never doubted that the agony I witnessed was anything less than the demon itself being seared by the name of the Father, the Son, the Holy Ghost.

We believed that the laying on of hands would heal the sick and raise the dead. We believed that there was only one road to Heaven and that it began at the altar. We raised our faces and spoke in tongues—a language known only to God and the angels. People called out their prophecies; women danced in the aisles, their hair set loose and flowing; men wept without shame. Those who were taken by the Spirit, *slain*, we said, collapsed to the floor, and we covered them with clean linens where they lay trembling and murmuring their delirious joy. Only in the church were we allowed so much release, such pure physical and emotional exhilaration. Perhaps this is why my parents, weaned on the dry teat of inexpression, found their greatest joy in those hours of praise.

We broke the bread that was the Body and drank the dark liquid that was the Blood of Christ. To consume the Eucharist with anything less than a pure mind and heart was unforgivable, and each communion, I searched my soul for some remaining sin. If I chose to let the plate go by, my secret trespass would be apparent to those around me. If I chose to partake, I might be doomed to eternity in Hell.

Yet I could not forego the ritual—the miniature glasses of grape juice clinking against the pewter tray (wine was forbidden), the way they nested so snugly, each in its individual slot; the coin-sized wafer, thin as a page from my Bible. When I held the unleavened bread in my hand, waiting for the minister to repeat the words of Christ at the Last Supper, I could not feel its weight. But it was there, softening with moisture, adhering to my palm like a second skin.

As young as I was, I could not escape the seeming impossibility of my mortal predicament: Christ could descend at any moment, come to carry his chosen ones home, yet only those whose garments were white as snow would be caught up. The smallest lie kept hidden, the mildest jealousy left unconfessed, would be enough to stain us forever, mark us for passage to Hell. Yet we could never be flawless, doomed as we were to imperfection. Our only hope was the second-by-second policing of our bodies and minds. "Go and sin no more," Christ had said. But how could we not? We were as God had made us—all sinners in His eyes.

As a woman, doubly cursed, my greatest hope was to find a husband who would continue to lead and protect me as steadfastly as my own father did. To earn such a blessing, I must remain pure of heart and body. The evil that might tempt me was everywhere, the preacher warned: in pool halls and movie theaters, bowling alleys and card rooms. Dancing was a sin, as were smoking, drinking, rock and roll, swimming with the opposite sex. I signed the Youth Pledge, swearing that I would not partake in any of these things. It seemed easy enough. I had never seen a pool table. The late-into-the-night pinochle marathons my parents had once staged with my aunts and uncles had ended when my relatives gave up the logging life and moved to Lewiston. The nearest movie theater was a hundred-mile round trip. It would not be until I had children of my own that I saw *Fantasia*, which, with its wizardry and enchanted brooms, embodied our belief in black magic. *Snow White*, *Cinderella*, *Old Yeller*—all off limits, all part of the American childhood that was not mine and would never be.

Television in and of itself was not a sin, but we did not have one and could not have received the distant signals anyway. When I visited my grandmother Nan, who had moved with my new step-grandfather to Lewiston, my parents were vigilant: *Gilligan's Island* was acceptable; *Bewitched*, with its nose-twitching sorceress, was not. Only after my parents were gone would my grandmother allow me to watch *Dark Shadows*, a Gothic soap opera complete with werewolves and vampires. I fell madly in love with the resident Transylvanian, Barnabas Collins, whose tragic and

noble desire to resist his thirst for blood seemed to embody
the human condition: in order to regain his soul, he must
deny his body its pleasure.

IT WASN'T UNTIL THE ARRIVAL of the new preacher and
his family that I came to understand such visceral desire. By
1968, the year the Langs took over pastorship of our church,
the last of my uncles had taken his wife and children and
moved to the city. We claimed Brother and Sister Lang, their
two sons and one daughter, as kin.

There were long sessions of Bible study and sermons, midday suppers of fried deer meat and mashed potatoes, the
grown-ups laughing and happy, the children wading the
creek or hunting squirrels in the meadow. In the hours after
evening service, I would sit in the parsonage stairway with
Luke—at thirteen the preacher's youngest son. Tall and lean,
with blue eyes and full lips, he was handsome enough to turn
any girl's head, and in the feel of his hand stroking my knee,
I came to an awareness of a truer temptation, too sweet not
to be sin. Yet even as I prayed for forgiveness, I longed to be
next to him, longed for the pleasure his closeness might
bring.

What little I knew of sex had come to me via school-yard
rumors and from a single book my mother handed to me a
few months before I turned twelve, although what it had to
say about my rapidly maturing body I'd already learned, and
what it had to say about intercourse was, *Don't.* Mostly I
heard about sex in the dire warnings against it. Kissing
would lead to petting, and petting was going-too-far and

might lead to going-all-the-way. This I knew from the endless lectures on the subject given by our Sunday-school teachers and the preachers themselves. They seemed, in fact,
obsessed with man and woman's desire for each other, and I
came to understand that all other wide and crooked roads led
to this one intersection: the illicit coming together of the
sexes outside the marriage bed. Drinking led to fornication
and adultery, as did going to pool halls, bowling alleys, and
movie theaters. Rock and roll was nothing more than an excuse to bump and grind: the beat—the hard-driving insistence of the drums and guitars, urging us back to our animal
desires, our savage roots—told it all. Anything that throbbed
or pulsed, shimmied in the darkness, was there for one reason
and one reason only: to lure our souls away from Heaven, to
fill the coffers of Hell.

During those long Sundays of church and covered-dish so-
cials and hours spent in the stairway with Luke, I never
thought to question this truth. I believed that, should Christ
return while I sat with the preacher's son, his fingers brushing my thigh, I would be doomed. No matter how much my
father had encouraged me to think for myself, I knew that to
question moral law was to doubt, to doubt was a weakness in
faith, and faith was everything. The answers were all there,
in the King James Bible: "There hath no temptation taken
you but that which is common to man." I prayed that God
give me strength to resist the new feelings flaring within me,
feelings that I believed arose not from the physical maturation of my body or from my elemental need for Luke's attention but from my ancestral transgression: it was Satan who
whispered in my ear so that I in my weakness would take

with me this other soul, whose only excuse was the man's natural and predictable passion for a woman made easy by sin.

AT SCHOOL, in the aging brick building that smelled of sour wool and paste, I felt protected by the innocence of my peers, few of whom seemed yet aware of their own sure damnation. I prayed over my sack lunch while the other children nibbled their cheese sandwiches in teacher-imposed silence, yet I never felt marginalized by my habits and appearance. There were so few of us, each with his or her eccentricities: Terry wet the bed and bit her nails to bloody stubs; Linda was a Jehovah's Witness, worse than any religion I could imagine, since they didn't celebrate birthdays or Christmas; Gordon's father was a drunk; Janet's mother cried at the PTA meetings, but no one knew why. Whatever group designations and boundaries might later form were not yet present my last year in the woods, when I met my sixth-grade friends at the monkey bars, tied my sweater around the steel pipe, and twirled myself into a dizzy freedom I have not known since.

I, like my friends, was the child of a logger, that was all. We did not have neighborhoods. We did not have blocks. We had *in-town* and *out-of-town*. We had camps and settlements and a new development built by Potlatch Forest Industries to house its workers. Some of our parents stayed home at night; some went to the bars, where they drank and danced and, more than once, shot one another to death in fits of jealous rage. Some were Protestant, some Catholic, some knew no religion at all. My schoolmates did not care that I had been gifted with the power of healing, that the visiting evangelist had announced it to the congregation, that I felt the heat come rushing to my hands whenever I touched the sick.

Everyone was struggling to get by, keep up, stay ahead. Simple survival bound us together, and when the sheriff or supervisor knocked on the front door with his hat in his hands, each wife felt her heart leave her. Injury and death came too often, brothers and sons and husbands caught by a barber-chaired hemlock, crushed by a loader, cut by a saw. My great-uncle was killed by a felled tree; the sawyer did not know he was near. When my grandmother remarried, it was to a man known as the Little Giant, a Norwegian logger who, only months after the wedding, was crushed by a load of logs. Although he survived, the damage to his brain left him doddering and disabled. My father ruptured a vertebra after tripping backward over a half-hidden stump, then endured several operations and months in a body cast before returning to the woods. Yet he loved his life there, and my mother loved him, and so we stayed, ferrying our meager belongings from one camp to the next, sometimes renting a house in Pierce, until 1969, when we took up residence in Dogpatch, in the line shack of my dead uncle.

It was there, in the spring of 1970, in that hollow where I turned twelve, that a brilliant light roused my father from sleep—the presence and voice of God, he believed, telling him we must go and never come back, away from that land in which we had made for ourselves a good life. It was the answer my father had been questing for: what could he offer his god? He had no desire for money or material things. He didn't drink or dance or lust after other women. He was poor in the eyes of men but rich with happiness in the life he had chosen: he had a lovely wife who shared his bed and beliefs; his children were strong and healthy; he rose each morning pleased with the light, savoring his work in the woods. What then? What could he give up as a token of his commitment to God?

He locked himself in the root cellar, intending to fast and pray for forty days and forty nights. It was his quest, his spiritual journey inward toward greater understanding. I often wonder what would have happened if he hadn't been interrupted by the surprise arrival of my youngest uncle and his family, who could only interpret my father's actions as verging on insane. He'd gone too far, some people thought, alarmed by my father's self-dependency and direction.

What I've come to understand is that it was his life in the woods that my father loved more than anything—more, even, than his wife and children; he has told me so. He had found his haven there, his safety and his comfort—the very things my father believed he must sacrifice.

Within days, we had left it all behind: the elk, the coyotes who wove their song through the forest. The raccoons had one last go at our garbage; the pack rats took what baubles they could from the cupboards and closets. I carried from that house in the wilderness a box of books, a suitcase of dolls I'd outgrown, the Bible given to me by our pastor and his family for my twelfth birthday.

I believed that the Bible would be my map through the world, a journal of warning and direction. As we drove the narrow road, past the logging camps and small settlements, across the Weippe Prairie, down the Greer Grade to the Clearwater River, I held it in my lap, feeling a loss I could not make sense of. I thought it was the boy that I missed, the preacher's son. I believed he would someday be my husband, that I would save myself for him, keep myself pure. With my mother's ballpoint pen, I wrote his name again and again in the palm of my hand as we followed the Clearwater toward the city of Lewiston one hundred miles west, down the same highway my mother had driven to reach the hospital in which I was born.

When we passed the dam at Ahsahka, I studied the giant flatness of its face: in less than a year its construction would be complete, the water that flowed past our camps gathering at its base, turning back on itself, flooding the North Fork beneath fifty miles of manmade lake. Already the good smells were gone—fresh-cut cedar, wood smoke from the shadowed houses, the late wild cherry, the early syringa. At Spalding, where the Nez Perce had listened to the missionaries' words, where some had begun to believe, we could already see the brown pall that covered Lewiston and crept up the valley floor. I held my nose against the sulfuric stench of the Potlatch pulp-and-paper mill. Red lights winked from its smokestacks, high above the perpetual light of its industry.

The ink in my palm bled into long blue lines, the boy's name a smudged tattoo. I opened my Bible: "I am the way, the truth, and the life." I closed my eyes, and the stars, for a moment, were there, fading, then gone before I could name them.

4 IT MIGHT HAVE BEEN A GOOD LIFE IN Lewiston, except for what went wrong. My grandmother was there, and we took shelter with her until my father could find work. My step-grandfather had been killed the year before, run over by a drunk driver while peddling ointment and spices, and now the care of their one-acre lot had fallen to Nan, twice widowed. She was our anchor, our point of stability, bedding us down beneath thick quilts, feeding us the potatoes and pot roast she believed would sustain us through anything.

Nan was a small woman, dark-haired, with eyes the color of smoke. Her greatest delight lay in her grandchildren, and I enjoyed long hours of her company and attention, playing checkers, watching forbidden TV shows, helping her in her meticulous rounds of housecleaning. That summer I shared her bed, wondrously soothed by the room's pale lavender paint and sacheted pillows. She said two of the four walls were mine to decorate, and so I hung torn-out pages from *Teen Magazine* on my side: Davy Jones and Bobby Sherman, a group photo of the Partridge Family. My parents allowed this, an indulgence less of my particular whims, I think, than of my grandmother's: above her side of the headboard she'd taped a toothy Engelbert Humperdinck.

Each night I watched as she wrapped her beauty-shop hairdo in tissue paper, rubbed her feet and hands with Jergens. I would fall asleep to her quietly singing "Good Night, Irene," comforted by her warm presence and soft perfume, while above us the airplanes flew low, headed for the runway a few blocks south. I would listen to the resonant thrum of engines, an unfamiliar and exotic sound, and I would try to imagine such travel, being held aloft by nothing but air. The thought would quicken my pulse, and I would burrow deeper beneath the covers, grateful for the touch of my grandmother's feet against mine, the whisper of her nightly prayers.

THERE WAS ANOTHER hard-timer in that house, below us in the downstairs bedroom. He was the son of my dead step-grandfather, and I called him Uncle, but I hardly knew him. Whenever he emerged, beetle-browed and growly, my brother and I gave him wide berth. Only when he left on some mysterious errand did I venture down into his corner room with its walls of painted concrete and its single, high window opened to air the musty smell.

Often it was my girl cousin Les, a year my junior, who accompanied me, who didn't need to be dared. Meeting her for the first time may be my oldest memory: my uncle, her new stepfather, carrying in his arms a little girl of two, white-blond hair and green eyes. My being a year older than she was gave me the only advantage I would ever have over Les.

She ran faster, hit harder, bit deeper than any other child I knew. She won basketball free-throw contests when girls were not supposed to compete, set records in the one-hundred-yard dash, alternately pampered and beat her huge stallion, Smokey, and broke the hearts of any number of boys whose affections she relentlessly trashed.

While my grandmother took her afternoon nap, we would sneak to the basement and begin our sleuthing, uncovering clues as to the life of our fearsome relative. What we found was a wooden wardrobe, several shirts pressed into neatness by Nan, a pair of black wingtips. In the bureau drawer was a pocket watch, matchbooks advertising various bars, important-looking papers, several handkerchiefs, shoestrings, bottle openers, military insignia, and a fistful of foreign coins. Next to the metal bedstead, in the magazine rack made of black iron, we discovered something far removed from the air-brushed portraits of teen idols hanging on the walls in the room above our heads: copies of *True Detective* and *True Crime*, on their covers the colored illustrations of women clad in slips and garters, hands to their mouths to stifle the scream, their eyes wide and focused on the dark male figure in the doorway.

There were other magazines, too, but instead of drawings, they had black-and-white photographs. In my mind's eye, I can no longer see the nude bodies or the settings or anything else that appeared in the smudgy pages—nothing except the black bars of ink covering the eyes, which I understood were meant to shield the men and women from shame, the shame I myself felt as Les and I lay on our uncle's high-sprung bed, reading in the basement's cool light, our skin tingling, our hearts racing with fear that we'd be caught.

It was there, in the room shut off from the drowsy heat of a summer afternoon, that Les and I found the book. On its cover was a woman, sitting on a chair, bound and gagged. Behind her, the men were dark and menacing silhouettes, shades of gray, sharp blue lines, black eyes and mouths. Les and I took turns reading the details aloud, how the rich, spoiled virgin had been kidnapped and held for ransom, how her captors raped her repeatedly and in all ways, how she had hated it at first, then how she came to want it more than anything. How foolish and childish she had been! Now she knew some part of herself she had never known before. She understood her truest nature.

And it must be true because I was dizzy with the buzz in my ears, the ache between my legs, and I knew it was sin and that sin came from what we should not know and feel.

Les and I read until we had memorized the most graphic pages, and then we foraged again and found another such book—the supposed diary of a Hong Kong madam. Whereas the first paperback taught us of a woman's desperate need to be dominated, the second taught us how a woman might please a man: with her knowledge of sexual secrets, her store of coveted tricks.

I had no context for the emotions and physical yearnings the books incited, no one to ask or tell, no one who would not be horrified, who would not punish. I could never bear the shame of confession, nor could I deny that dark part of me that wanted, more than anything, to protect the books from confiscation.

It was a dividing point for me—between what I had not known and now knew, between what I feared and what I longed for. My new knowledge separated me from my mother and father, from my grandmother, from my brother, whose face had not yet taken on the mask of guarded transgression. It was as though I were permanently stained, as though some part of me had gone underground.

Les and I made a pact that we would not tell anyone, ever. We cut our fingers with our uncle's razor and swore blood truth. Now we were more sisters than cousins, and over the next decade, our lives would be informed and directed by those stories in ways we could not then imagine. By the time I left my grandmother's house that summer, I possessed a knowledge of sexual deviation that would stun my friends years into the future. When they asked me how I knew, I would smile and shrug, thinking how it had always been with me, somewhere near the beginning, when I had first understood that women want what men give, that what power I might possess could be found by mastery of the erotic, that in submission lay the greatest pleasure of all.

But I could not submit—not then, not later, not when it was what my father demanded of me, not even when I believed it was what I must give or else be destroyed. Always, some part of me resisted. Yet even as I prided myself on the strength of my will and fierce independence, I heard the whisper, the oldest voice telling me that my time would come, that my woman's fate would someday find me.

BY AUGUST 1970 my father had found nighttime work in Lewiston as a truck driver, hauling sawdust and chips, two or three trips upriver, back to that land we had left, where the smaller mills would load his trailer with wood scraps, which he carried back down to Potlatch, Inc., to be ground and bleached and pressed into tissue paper and cardboard.

We left my grandmother's and moved into a white, hacienda-style house with a patio and goldfish pond instead of a meadow and creek outside the door. It was more than we could afford, but my mother had swung a deal, bartering paint and yard work for low rent. I'd never lived in such a grand house, with a laundry chute and multiple toilets. The air inside felt hollow, the rooms too large and numerous for our sparse furnishings; our voices echoed from the walls. We could have danced in those rooms, but my father came home weary, his back stiff with the pain of hours behind the wheel, and I was too old to waltz atop his feet. I preferred to keep to my bedroom, where I secretly listened to the local rock-and-roll station and danced solo in front of my dresser mirror, imitating the miniskirted teenagers I'd watched on *American Bandstand,* moving my hips, my shoulders, gesturing seductively to my phantom love.

The house's narrow kitchen provided the greatest sense of intimacy. Outside its single window, I could see nothing but the stark flatness of the neighbors' house, only a few feet away, but above the sink my mother had pinned the trailing philodendron she tended from house to house, its variegated leaves shined each week with a wash of canned milk and water, its occasional cuttings rooted in jars on the sill.

Through the kitchen was the breakfast nook, the most privileged and exotic of the rooms, just large enough for a small and elegant table, had we one, but empty except for the telephone, which nested in its own miniature grotto. Around the room's far wall ran a window seat, on which I could lie and study the grapevines growing rampant across the green-house roof.

We spent only one year in that house, but I remember it as a time of sweetness and light, the kitchen steamy with boiling water and great pots of stewing grapes. I remember my mother, her fine hair caught up with a scarf, stray curls at her neck and temples. I helped her scald the little Ball jars, rings, and lids, dissolve the pectin, melt the paraffin. Pounds of sugar, a plastic lemon full of concentrate from which I sucked the last jaw-locking drops, a cone-shaped sieve and a wooden pestle worn smooth by generations of hands. I loved the efficiency and assemblage, and I loved the closeness of my mother, who was just turning thirty. There was not yet so much distance between us that we could not share such space and movement. In the years to come I would look back and remember the jars filled with syrupy fruit, the wax floated on top, the lids pinging as they sealed, the deep purple juice that stained our mouths black; I would remember the feeling of safety and sureness and provision and wonder when that closeness had been lost.

OVER THE NEXT YEAR, I watched as my father rose in the evening, took his meal, collected his calfskin gloves and lunch pail and walked into the darkness. Mornings, just as Greg and I woke for school, my father would come back through the door, bringing with him the remembered smells of diesel and cedar but none of the joy he once brought home from the wilderness.

It was all different. The water we drank was chlorinated,

our meat wrapped in Styrofoam and plastic. Our church, the Assembly of God, was progressive, allowing women to wear makeup and pants. My mother took a job checking groceries at McPherson's; my brother began playing ball. Sometimes, when I came home from school, I was alone, except for my father dreaming in his shaded room. On still afternoons I would lie on the couch and sleep, startled when I woke to find my father in his chair, eating Saltines and cheese, reading his Bible, watching me.

We were in the world, and the world would destroy us. It was out there, waiting, biding its time. There were hippies and drug dealers, sex maniacs and pimps, Communists and big-city gangs. Even in Idaho, kids were being lured away by marijuana and LSD, flower power and peace marches. My father became more vigilant. What I *could* do was participate in church activities, go to school, and be with my family. What I couldn't do was join drill team or play girls' basketball, which required the wearing of indecent clothes. After I came back from a football game one evening, disoriented by the sensory overload of floodlights and the pep band's deafening blare, my parents were frightened. Better that I remain at home, under supervision. The risks were simply too great.

Each schoolday, I walked the few blocks to Jenifer Junior High, where the girls wore fishnet stockings and blue eyeshadow, where the high school boys hung out in their GTO's and Barracudas, smoking Marlboros and listening to Casey Kasem play the Top 40. For the first time in my life, I saw myself as others must: a plain-faced girl in home-sewn clothes, doing what was expected of her. I went to church, I went to school. I brought home A's and teachers' commendations. I risked nothing, while all around me the world was on fire: Woodstock, Vietnam, Kent State, Haight-Ashbury. Race riots and Agent Orange. The Rolling Stones, Jimi Hendrix, Janis Joplin, the Who. Men were burning their draft cards, women were burning their bras. Sin, sin everywhere, just as the Bible had warned, and yet, like Lot's wife, I could not quit looking, hungry for one last glimpse before the judgment of the Lord descended.

A freak, I thought. There were so few others like me. Even the girls with whom I attended church were allowed to wear nylons while I trudged along in my knee socks, the hem of my dress brushing my calves. No one in my class understood why I could not go to the after-school dances held in the cafeteria, or why the Liberty Theater was taboo. Where once I had proudly borne witness to my faith, knocking on doors, spreading the Gospel, I was now too embarrassed to explain why I couldn't join drill team, why I turned down invitations for birthday parties at the skating rink. Soon, even the nicest and most compassionate girls quit asking me to join them.

But there was another group, teenagers who themselves had been marginalized, rejected. Many of them were kids from the Northwest Idaho Children's Home, an orphanage and detention center for those with nowhere else to go. They were the ones who spent their lunch period in the empty lot across the street from school, cupping their Marlboros, slouching in their ragged jackets and faded jeans. They were the ones who took me in, placed the cigarette in my fingers, ridiculed those who had taunted me.

My father sensed my growing frustration, caught the rise of rebellion in my voice. The only response he knew was to take in rein, bear down harder, lock all the doors and bar escape. I began skipping school to meet my friends at the river, where we cajoled the railroad hoboes into sharing their wine, where we pushed ourselves into the swift water on packing-crate rafts and wished for the current to take us.

I no longer believed in who I was, or why. Nothing made sense except my need to reach out and taste the forbidden. I knew what punishment my acts would bring, but I no longer cared. Better to risk body and soul than to be imprisoned by the tyrannical laws my father and the church imposed. I was hungry for a world I had never known, a world held at bay by the mountains and the trees, by my parents, who meant only to save me. I spent my fourteenth year in basements and back alleys, in the blue glow of black lights, listening to Led Zeppelin, learning how to French-kiss, smoking dope, dropping mescaline, waiting for a vision that might change it all.

IN THE LATE SPRING OF 1972, instead of walking home after school, I met a girlfriend with whom I had made my plans to escape. We would *run away*, that magical phrase that promised to sever all ties to my old life, connect me to the new. We'd catch a ride with an older guy I'd never met who specialized in such underground relocations, ferrying discontent teenagers across the state line for little more, we'd heard, than the price of a doobie.

I never made it to the new land, to California—that oasis of freedom to which my friends and I were headed. My parents found me before I'd even left Lewiston, hiding in the closet of my friend's mother—a humiliation I could hardly bear. But they could do no more. My heart was hardened, my conscience seared. Their only hope, they believed, was to send me away to live with the Langs, our former preacher and his family, who, like us, had traveled from the woods and now lived in Spokane.

I left Lewiston that summer knowing that all through the hot days of July and the late heat of August, my friends would smoke pot and listen to Black Sabbath and swallow the tiny tabs of Windowpane and Orange Sunshine; they would sprawl across the goal line of the empty football field to watch the moon rise, see it burst like a yellow balloon. They would close their eyes and taste butter on their tongues. They would eat my share of the sky—while I was stripped of my beads and makeup and given a bed in the Langs' upstairs hallway. While I was under supervision day and night, allowed to go nowhere alone lest I flee. While I hoarded the last of my cigarettes and swore my hatred of God and man. I watched Luke, the preacher's son, now sixteen, walk by me as though I were invisible, a chair in the corner, a ghost in his house. I remembered his hands between my knees, the dark stairwell we hid in, my adolescent shame and pleasure, there in the parsonage, there in the woods.

I tried to stay awake at night, to tend the hard knob of bitterness in my chest, because I hated to wake in the morning and feel, in that moment just before awareness, that girl I once had been take up residence in my body. She was the one who awakened with her eyes and mouth open, as though whatever might greet her came pleasant and sweet. I'd close my eyes, open them again, and she'd be gone, back to the closet I had made for her, back to where her softness could not be touched.

———

THE LANGS reminded me of what I had once loved, of how simple things were when there was only one way. Over the course of that summer, I felt the fabric of who I was begin to tear. There came a time when I could no longer remember why it was I resisted, what I hoped to save myself from. I was isolated from my friends and family, but there was something else that wore at my resistance. It promised peace. It offered forgiveness. It whispered that I would never be free if I didn't let go, give in.

I remember how I lay on the floor of my narrow room and cried, then prayed. I felt the weight that was all my sins and worries and cares press me down, then fall away. It happens just this way: one moment, the horrid drunkenness of a life not right, of a soul bloated by neglect and transgression; the next, a feeling of lightness and sharp cleansing. Simply by letting go of my will, my stubborn refusal to submit, I'd been unbound, reborn into the Kingdom of God.

When I came to the breakfast table that morning, those people who had only tolerated my presence welcomed me with open arms. We joined hands above the scrambled eggs and bacon and gave thanks for my salvation. Beneath the linen cloth, I felt the shuffle of feet against mine, the brush of an ankle, and opened my eyes to the eyes of Luke. He smiled, and I was infused with pleasure. Along with everlasting life, I had earned this reward: the approval of the man I now loved.

That pleasure instilled in me a desire to do only good. I was redeemed, and for the price of my soul's purchase I offered up daily prayers, busy hands, a chaste body and clean mind. I imagined how grateful my parents would be when they saw their daughter come back from the grave. I would prove to them how loving, how honest I could be. I would mend the wounds I had caused.

I lengthened my skirts, scrubbed my face pink. I remembered to lower my eyes in modesty, to fold my hands neatly in the pleat of my lap. Was this what Luke had been waiting for? He might not have touched me otherwise, had I remained something unclean, unholy, unworthy of his desire. When he came to me deep in the night, I resisted because I knew it was what might prove my chastity, make him want to keep me. I felt his jaw tighten, the tendons of his arms hard against my breasts. When he went no further but pushed me away, then began to laugh, I breathed out a prayer of thanks. Now, I must continue to withstand, repel his advances because that is what he really wanted of me—it was the test, the fire. It was the unmarried woman's duty, she who was charged with countering, tempering, molding the man's instinctual passion. In my bed, even as I grieved for the loss of his touch, I swore I would remain pure, a gift for the husband I believed he would be.

I believed that if I lived by the Book, the world would fall into place, and I could regain that peace I had lost. I was wrong. What happened at the end of that summer would define the story I told myself of faith, love, and betrayal for years to come; it would rend my sense of who I was into pieces I still struggle to fit together.

Something began to shift in that house, something I sensed but could not speak, even to myself. I saw it in the way the Langs addressed me, or didn't, in the way they let their eyes slide away from my face. Perhaps the threat of who I was remained; even though I had shed the skin of my former self, I still carried with me the stink of the purgatory I had once inhabited.

I became more diligent in my chores, more dedicated in my prayers and fasting, until one day Sister Lang confronted me. I was evil, she said, a harlot whom the demons had followed: she and Brother Lang had heard them, shuffling in the closets, wallowing beneath the beds. She said she knew what I had done: seduced not her son but her son-in-law in the very church that had saved me, in the sacristy, the most holy of chambers.

I could not convince her that none of this was true. There was no way for me to make sense of her lies, nor of the way they then shunned me. In their faces turned away, I saw what I was, what I must always be.

I was kept in those rooms until the end of the summer when my parents came for me. Instead of a slouching teenager who spat her anger, what they found was that good girl I had once been, dressed in modest clothing, nodding politely, quick to attend to her father's wishes. How could it not be the miracle for which they had so diligently prayed? They knew nothing of my life there except that I had been transformed back into the daughter they remembered, before things went bad, before the Devil whispered my name.

When, on the drive from Spokane to Lewiston, I attempted in some way to articulate what had taken place, my mother responded with silence, my father with a single, oblique comment: "I was afraid that something like this might happen."

Although I might have interpreted my father's statement

as a kind of acknowledgment of the Langs' culpability, what I believed was that the Langs' rejection was my punishment, that I had earned it with my willfulness and rebellion. Back in our church at Lewiston, I sat straight in my pew beside my family and sang, "I want Thee forever to ransom my soul." I sang, "I shall be whiter than snow." When the sermon ended, I knelt at the altar for hours until my body weakened and I lay on the floor with others, whispering my plea, praying for more.

MY PARENTS AND I never talked about what happened that summer. The distance between us was loud with what we could not say—words of anger, words of love. My relationship with my father seemed to exist only through proxy. If I needed permission to date or stay late after church, it was my mother I queried, who then asked my father and relayed his yes or no.

Time not spent at school or church I filled with books, their pages softening the silence. I read about the cowboy Shane and Loki, the Norse god of mischief. I read *The Martian Chronicles* and *1984*. I suffered through the cruelties visited upon Oliver Twist by the industrial machine. One literature teacher rewarded my interest by giving me the task of screening books for the class library, and so, before my parents could find out, I'd read my way through *A Clockwork Orange*, *Go Ask Alice*, and *Everything You Always Wanted to Know About Sex but Were Afraid to Ask*.

I borrowed from the county library in methodical fashion: I started at the beginning of the fiction shelves and checked out three books at a time, working my way through science fiction (the spines with their yellow rocket ships and nuclear atoms), through fantasy and mystery, classics and contemporary. I discovered the stories of the Holocaust; I read about Sybil and her umpteen personalities.

I paid no attention to the names of authors—the stories were what mattered. I read Judith Krantz and Richard Bach with the same rapt attention I gave Roth and Bellow. I liked *Jonathan Livingston Seagull*, and so the librarian gave me Castaneda. Mysticism fascinated me: Nostradamus and Black Elk, Philippine faith healers, African fire walkers, Uri Geller, who could twist a fork with nothing more than the power of his mind. But this was witchcraft, and so I hid the books in the folds of my sweaters, secreted them away between *Little Women* and *The Cross and the Switchblade*.

What I wanted was someone to share this with, someone who could talk with me about things both common and extraordinary. I'd made few friends since my conversion: others in our youth group still eyed me with suspicion, and I was not sure where I fit into their circle. Although I had confessed my sins and been forgiven, my transgressions stayed with me like an ember bedded in ash: who knew what might fan that fire, cause it to spread and inflame those who stood too close? My intimacy with the world set me apart from those whose pages in the Book of Life remained unsullied.

As much as I longed to regain that place of purity, I had little tolerance for the simple platitudes and condemnations the church handed down. Throughout the calls for Catholics to forsake their idolatry and know the true God, for women to turn deaf ears to promoters of the ERA who wanted only to enslave them, for the fornicators and adulterers and the nearly unmentionable Sodomites to forego their evil ways before the Day of Judgment fell upon them, I felt my resistance rise, and perhaps it was this that I believed set me apart—my innate unwillingness to simply believe, agree, accept. I kept silent, for to question might imply that my allegiance lay with the Enemy.

Instead of lashing out, I drove my rebellion underground, so deep that even I forgot it was there. Its eruptions were minor compared with the wholesale rejection I'd practiced before, and I believed I might survive this way, presenting my shining surface for inspection while beneath ran the currents of my desire for knowledge, for freedom to explore and experience and entertain the endless possibilities contained in my body and mind.

Each night I prayed for the humility to accept my station, to lay down my armor and weapons and quit fighting, let go that inherent and overwhelming drive I felt to set my own course, fly into the face of my predetermined fate. I knew that to continue in my obstinacy would once again lead me down the path to destruction. I must be docile, pliant, willing to bend. I must be a dutiful daughter, make of myself a worthy wife. Above all, I must, for the length of my woman's life, give myself over to the direction of another.

THE FALL OF MY FRESHMAN YEAR in high school, I came to believe that what held my greatest allegiance was not my family or my church but Tom, a thin, fair-haired boy who had begun his courtship while holding my hand during prayer, so that, even now, when I remember my voice rising in praise that early September, I feel the tingle of something new about to happen, something sparking, traveling my knuckles, settling light and electric beneath my breastbone.

He was the son of a deacon, a good boy a year older than I was who didn't smoke or drink or cuss, who, like me, wore glasses and spent too much time reading. We began sitting together during Sunday school, walking hand in hand from the foyer. Hand-holding in and of itself was not a sin, but, we'd been warned, it could lead to disastrous things. (I still have several of the "hand-holding sticks" various young suitors carved for me at church camp, abiding by the rules set by our elders: the boy could hold one end, the girl the other, and in this way their flesh would not be tempted toward further engagement.)

Our parents were friends, and so there were afternoons when we were able to gaze at each other with great longing across the dinner table, and I began to believe that I might not survive more than a few hours away from Tom. My father, I knew, was watching me carefully: my overt preoccupation with a boy was new territory for both of us.

Could I go with Tom for a Coke after choir practice? Yes, my father said, as long as I returned home by the designated hour. Sundays after church, Tom took me to the gravel pit just south of Lewiston, where we fired round after round from his .22 revolver. The further I stood from the target, the more shots I placed in the tightest space, the more he praised me. He taught me to load and unload, sight in, compensate for distance and trajectory. He bought a .357, and I learned to allow for greater recoil, the concussion through my wrists and shoulders.

Those long afternoons alone with Tom, hidden from the

road by a cirque of basalt, gave me my first taste of true freedom. The reflected warmth of the rock, the heavy gun in my
hands, Tom's soft words of direction and praise, the red-
tailed hawks winging lazy loops overhead—I felt both independent and protected, stronger, and strangely new.

Tom lived in a large house with his parents and numerous
siblings. As long as there were adults on the premises, my father said, I could go there, and I soon became a fixture at
Tom's dinner table, happy to be part of his raucous family, in
rooms that seemed vibrant with television and music—less
silent, less rigid than my own somber home. Tom and I spent
hours listening to the rock-and-roll albums I was not allowed
to possess, mesmerized by the flashing colored lights he had
wired to his speakers. We talked of things that, aboveground,
were taboo—the rumors and stories that fascinated us: the
symbolism of Paul's barefooted march across the Beatles'
Abbey Road album cover; the eery accurateness of my
cousin's Ouija board; the article I had read about epileptic
seizures bringing on visions. Though neither of us suffered
from the disorder, we wondered if Tom's chronic migraines
might not serve to bring on an otherworldly aura, transport
him to another plane.

It might have been there, in his bedroom, or perhaps in
the cold interior of his car, or even in the alley behind the
church, that we began to feel our virginal resolve weaken. It
was a sin to move beyond the feverish kissing that kept us oc-
cupied for long minutes in the parking lot's dark corner
while our parents chatted after evening service. Tom's hand
would find my breast, I would murmur that he mustn't, and
then he would profess to great misery and guilt, and we

would both pray for strength and forgiveness. I don't remember at what point the prayers quit working. I know that we were very young and very determined to save ourselves for marriage and that there came a moment when none of this was enough to smother the fire we had kindled in each other's body. We agonized at first, and then we didn't but simply began to allow ourselves the pleasure of consummation.

We rationalized and reasoned: we were in love; we would be married the moment I turned eighteen, if not before. We imagined illicit escapes and elopements. Tom gave me a thin gold ring in which a single diamond chip was embedded, a promise that we would soon be engaged. When I showed it to my mother, she shook her head, said it was too much, too soon.

"But you were married when you were sixteen," I argued. "Why should it be any different for me?"

"It just is, Kim. I didn't know any better."

This meant nothing to me. All I saw was hypocrisy, unjust criticism, and restriction. My father said only one thing: I must give the ring back. I could not imagine such infidelity, and so I hid the ring in my pockets and purse, slipped it on my finger the moment I left my parents' field of vision. I believed that nothing they could do would be punishment enough to separate me from Tom. He was the one with whom I could share every part of myself, the intimate who knew me better than any mother, father, or friend. We spent hours whispering our secrets, feeding ourselves to each other in bits and pieces, until we seemed less two people than a single, unified self. I was besotted by the intensity of Tom's attention, the way he kissed me, took my breath into his lungs, touched each hidden part of me. How could we not call this love?

It must have been apparent to everyone that what we were about was no longer simple infatuation but something bordering on obsession. My father's growing disapproval of the time we spent together only strengthened my resolve to remain loyal to my lover. Soon there was little I would not do to gain a few more minutes with Tom. We wove elaborate plans to meet, skipping school, dodging teachers, urging our friends to cover for us should our parents discover that we'd sneaked from the back pew during the minister's long-winded sermon. At one point Tom and another young man from the church consolidated their savings—enough to pay for one month's rent of an airless apartment beneath the eaves of a crumbling Victorian mansion—a place of privacy, where we could lie together and love without interruption.

The other boy and his girlfriend reserved the even days, Tom and I the odd. Tom presented the key to me as a gift, pleased with himself for daring such adult maneuvers. I was amazed and frightened by such risk. What if my father were to find out? How could I ever explain?

Tom interpreted my hesitation as an insult. He'd worked hard for the money, taken chances so that we could be together. I talked myself into believing that we deserved this hideaway, that the oppression of parents and church had driven us to take such a step, forced us to take our love into hiding.

But if the idea of such a retreat was romantic, the reality was not. I remember the lack of light and the cold darkness.

The rooms smelled of spoiled food and mildewed linens. There was a small wooden table and two chairs, a rough-edged counter, a rust-ridden sink. The bed was a thin mattress with blue-striped ticking, discolored with sweat and urine. When I told Tom that I could not lie on it, he scowled, then spread his shirt and coat to cover the most offensive stains. He was, I could tell, not happy with me. As I lay beneath him, I felt nothing of the liberation such space had promised. What I felt instead was disgust. How many others had lain in this same room, for an hour, a night? What kind of woman would come here? I felt cheap and dirty, as though the soiled bedding had bled onto my skin.

"You're ruining this," Tom said. He sat up, his shoulder blades sharp in the shadows of afternoon light.

"I'm sorry." I did not know what else to say. His anger made me feel as though I could not breathe. Men were dangerous if made angry. It was my job to soothe, to make things right. I placed the palm of my hand against his spine, let two fingers trace the vertebrae's path.

"I'm just a little nervous, that's all." I pulled gently at his arms. "I'm cold."

"Maybe I should just take you home."

"No," I said, "I want to stay here." I moved my hand across his back. "Next time I'll bring a blanket. We'll have a picnic lunch. We'll say we're going to the river." I imagined a checkered tablecloth, a Mason jar of dried flowers. Maybe I could sneak a sheet or two. Maybe I could find a curtain for the kitchen window, a rug for in front of the sink, bring softness and color to this place my lover had chosen. I thought of all the houses my mother had remade with little more than a swatch of gingham and a bucket of Pine-Sol.

"Maybe," I said, "I just need to learn how to *be* here, how to act."

"We can be whoever we want here. We can act however we want." He pulled me against him roughly. "There are no rules."

There was a new insistence in him. Before, our times together had held a certain balance—both of us eager, both of us taking, both of us giving. But this was different. Now our roles were more defined: he the taker, I the giver. I felt disconnected, separated from my body, unable to feel the rush and rise of blood, unable to focus on anything other than the fly-specked ceiling, the room's webbed corners, the bare bulb hung from its wire.

When he was done, we lay together, listening to the sounds of traffic, the distant whistle of the mill train, and I had a sudden sense of impending loss. What if Tom were to become impatient, tire of me? What if I no longer pleased him? I was fifteen, maybe sixteen years old, and already I was wondering how I could keep this man—how I might reshape my own desire to more convincingly reflect his, become the lake he might fall into, enchanted by his own image in the mirroring surface.

EVEN THOUGH HE MAY NOT HAVE KNOWN the intricacies of my relationship with Tom, there is no mystery to my father's reasons for doing what he could to keep me home. It was not simply the obvious intimacy between Tom and me that alarmed my father but something perhaps even more dangerous. My father saw what I could not: Tom's intensifying possessiveness, his demands that made my father's rules seem nearly enlightened.

Tom insisted that, as the man, it was he who should determine my boundaries, and one of those boundaries was that I could go nowhere without his attendance. If I could not be with him, Tom said, then he didn't want me with anybody, and I could only see this as a manifestation of his affection: wasn't this the way I had come to know all great love, through what it asked of me, through my adherence to the giver's conditions? My father's love, just like that of the Heavenly Father, necessitated that he guide and confine my behavior; I returned that love by concession and obedience. It was, I understood, for my own good.

Yet who would I obey? If I went against my father, I was grounded, left without recourse; if I attended a high school football game or a church prayer rally without Tom, he became enraged, ranted that I was a whore, threatened to abandon me.

Increasingly, my fear of Tom's disapproval outweighed the threat of my father's censure. I could, I believed, live without paternal love, but I could never survive losing Tom. What could I say or do that would prove to him my faithfulness, my allegiance? I pledged and promised, soothed him with words, touched him with my lips and fingers. I no longer thought of sin or damnation or even pleasure but instead wondered if this would be enough to win his tolerance and favor for a while longer, make him see that I was wholly his. Sex became something other, something more than a shared journey toward physical delight; it became a coin that I could use to buy back his approval.

I believed I had given every part of myself to Tom, yet his jealousy increased, as did his policing of my attire and activities. He hectored and harassed, his anger turning more and more menacing until one night he wrapped his fingers around my throat and I thought he would kill me.

Even then, it was he who ended the relationship, left me crying and hysterical, believing that I had not given enough, or taken enough, that somehow it was my fault that he'd turned mean. If I hadn't worn that dress, talked to those other boys, if I'd stayed home like he'd asked—weren't these the things I'd been taught would save a woman?

My parents were relieved, but I felt an enormous loss, not only of Tom but of some part of myself. I had thought I would marry this boy, but now I was alone and no longer a virgin—a state that forecasted despair for any woman who hoped to win an honest man. I was "ruined"—I had heard my mother and grandmother pronounce it of other women—and I envisioned a life of sorrowful decay and abandonment.

After Tom, there were other boys I believed I might love, and so I kept myself from them, thinking that to do so would shield my secret transgression and ensure their fidelity, win from them the respect and admiration such chastity attracted. Instead of approval, what my abstinence brought me was, at first, steady imploring, then anger and scorn. Why had I agreed to go out to a movie, for dinner, if I wasn't ready to give something in return? I was a prude, a prick tease, not worth their money and time. Some part of me—that part that Tom had tended so well—believed them. It seemed that no matter which path I chose, I was doomed to rejection.

———

THERE WAS ONE BOY whose romance undid me, remade me, broke me into even smaller pieces. Thane was a raven-haired athlete with a good arm and fast moves on the field. He had a steady girlfriend, but it didn't seem to matter. He offered a special kind of companionship: afternoons of television and popcorn; Saturdays spent sledding and drinking hot cocoa; evenings when he called for no other reason than to pick me up, take me to the park, and launch a new kite above the city.

After the tyranny of my relationship with Tom, Thane's childlike pleasure in the world and the fact that he demanded nothing of me was a gift. We were intimates but not lovers, and I cherished this, believing that it freed me somehow.

My father gave easier approval of my spending time with Thane. By all accounts, he was a respectable young man, liked by his teachers, admired by his peers, the shining star of numerous sporting events. He was polite and respectful, never surly or secretive. More often than not, there were others who accompanied us on our outings, groups of friends intent on a long evening of pizza and pinball. Such activities—ball games and pool parties, even the occasional movie rated G—were all new to me, and my father continued to surprise me with his acquiescence. Perhaps he had come to believe that this secular socializing might prevent the kind of fixation that had possessed me in my relationship with Tom.

I shared Thane's family dinners, came to the parties he held for his classmates—the boys and girls coupling up and finding the darkened back rooms of the basement, while, up-stairs, his parents—the adult supervision on whom my fa-ther's approval depended—watched *The Odd Couple* and mixed another gin fizz. I wasn't interested in the beer se-creted in beneath coats and book bags, nor did I care to let the other boys whisper me into the laundry room for an extended bout of French kissing, their zippered jeans grinding my hip-bones raw. I was not a cheerleader, already claimed by the team's top scorer, nor was I the plump girl in glasses who braced herself against the wall and lifted her sweater with-out hesitation, urging the boy to hurry. My choices were to stay and remain a part of the dim light and the music, or leave and go home, back to my solitary bed and the lacklus-ter night. I sat on the couch, paralyzed by my separateness, an unopened can of Coors warming in my hand, listening to America sing, "I've been through the desert on a horse with no name."

When a boy I hardly knew pinched my arm and asked me to dance, I hesitated, trying to remember the steps my father had taught me, trying to remember the ease of his lead.

"Like this," the boy said, and pressed my head against his shoulder, his arms raising my wrists to drape around his neck. We swayed in a small circle, and I breathed in the clean smell of his shirt, the complex odor of his skin, which made me feel animal and hungry and close to tears. He rocked me into the hallway, pushed open a door, then gathered me like a bride in his arms before laying me across the guest bed, musty with disuse.

"It's okay." He shushed my protests with his mouth. For a moment, the movement of his hands was a comfort, but then his patience with me thinned, his need became more urgent.

"Wait," I said, but he wouldn't, pummeling more than petting, burying his face in the softness below my ribs. When I pushed against him with the heels of my hands, said, "Stop," he covered my mouth, his breath heavy in my face.

"Be quiet. Someone might hear you."

I wrestled myself from beneath his weight, felt him roll away from me. "I don't want to do this," I said.

"Yes you do." He ran a finger down my arm, kissed my shoulder. I shivered, sat up. I could hear the music, the sound of other voices. He will hate me now, I thought, even as he smoothed his hair and left the bed, stepped out of the dark room and disappeared. Every time such closeness came, it ended in my feeling even more isolated and alone. If they all turned away, who would be left to love me?

It was not this boy whose affection I most craved, but that of the boy who rolled and moaned in the next room. I knew that Thane was with his girlfriend, but I could not forget how, only hours before, he had kissed me for the first time. Had he felt me hesitate, nearly give in, the second or third or thirteenth time he tried to touch my breast? I longed to hold him against me, even as I told myself that such contact would destroy whatever existed between us. Some nights I allowed myself to fantasize that Thane might actually fall in love with me and leave his girlfriend, that we would be married and have dark-haired babies, that as his wife I might regain a sense of my own decency and entitlement.

I listened to his voice rise and fall, the soft laughter of his girlfriend. I tucked my knees against my chest, rested my forehead against my arms. Thane didn't know the other side of me, how I could touch him and move him in ways his lover could not. And what if he did? What if I showed him?

What if he needed me in this way, came to me because I knew how to please him more than any other woman?

I shook my head in the dark. I did not want to be that girl anymore, the one who stole the book and its secrets, who abandoned herself to lust on a filthy bed. *Please let me be good, I prayed. Please let me be good.*

THE NEXT WEEK was Thane's birthday, and I had a gift for him—a Bible with his name embossed in gold. After much prodding on my part, he had begun attending church, sitting beside me in the pew, bowing his head in prayer. This was the way it should be. My testimony had brought him closer to his own salvation, and if he were saved, then so was I.

We were alone in his basement when he unwrapped the Bible, laid it aside, then pushed me down amid the colorful paper and ribbons. I laughed at first but then saw that he was not teasing. He pinned my arms above my head, held me with his weight. I remember how, at some point, I quit struggling, how I could not bear my own rising sense of helplessness or his growing brutality, how I turned my head so that I would not have to see who he had become, how it was easier to simply stop knowing and feeling and let that frantic part of me drift away.

Perhaps it was pity he felt for me then, or fear for his own soul, the slackness of my body beneath his that made him stop. I rolled to my knees, smoothed my clothes, focused my eyes on the wall behind him. "I'll see you tomorrow," I said. Even as I spoke, I let what had just happened float like bits of ash into the air around us. We would not have to remember, would we? No one would have to know, no one would have to see the bracelet of bruises circling each wrist.

I drove my car down the backstreets, holding to the edge of the city. The reds and oranges of fall were crisp against the pale blue sky, the stones in the cemetery angled and sharp as blades. Everything was so defined, distinct in its place, yet I felt as though I had no borders, as though my skin had begun to dissolve, as though I were the watercolor painting drawn by a child, bleeding across the lines.

I was grateful for the emptiness of my house, the bathwater so hot I gritted my teeth to bear it. I did not think about what would happen next but gave myself to the weightlessness of water, to the nebulous cloud of steam and sleep, waking only to add more heat, to open the drain and let the cold flow away.

When Thane called several days later, he was crying. "I'm so sorry," he said. "Please."

Charity, forgiveness, compassion—I thought of all these things, Christ's words of direction. I thought of the leather-bound book he held in his hands, even then, as we talked and made our plans to meet again, and I thought that this must have been what I had wanted all along, and that I could not blame him for anything.

SOMETHING BROKE in me then—I cannot say what or why exactly, except that the restrictions I had placed on myself seemed suddenly pointless and impossible. When I met Thane at his house, I didn't feel anger or disgust or betrayal; I felt nothing I can remember except a kind of disconnectedness, as though my world were being orchestrated in a way I could not control. I could lock myself in my house, sit pale and unsullied behind my father's protective door, or I could go into the world, but I had begun to see the truth in my father's teachings: to step through that passageway was to walk into the den of the lion.

I knew that I could never sacrifice myself to the life of a nun. There was too much I wanted to know, do, see. This, then, was the path I chose, knowing what dues would be demanded of me. There seemed no other way.

When Thane hid his face in shame, I stroked the bareness below his earlobe. I kissed the crown of his head, the thin ridge of his shoulder. How could I be angry, turn him away—he with his passion and humility, his grief-stricken face? *Here,* I said, and wrapped my arms around him, comforting, accepting that it was I who had brought him to this, after all, and that now I must be steadfast and strong so that he might rise and go on. My own penance was to do what he asked of me. Instead of him becoming the romantic teenage boyfriend I longed for, I became the secret lover he had fantasized. Instead of flying kites and going to matinees, we met for the moments he might take his pleasure before he left to share the evening with his truer love, and I returned to the house of my father, who slept the daylight hours and drove until dawn. Sometimes, during the course of our entrances and exits, my father and I met in the doorway, nodding our hellos or good-byes, something gone wrong between us, and no words to help understand why.

I ATTENDED CHURCH five times a week, kept up my grades, and worked after school at a local pharmacy. I had friends and all the activities a Christian-bookstore calendar could hold. My daily life must have appeared ordinary enough to my family, although, except for those drives to and from the Assembly of God and the occasional Sunday dinner, there seemed little connection between us.

My father had all but disappeared, sinking deeper into his thoughts, his head weaving over the pages of his Bible, his blue eyes hazy with hours of reading. I may have thought him at peace, although I know better now, having come to understand how much our trek out of the wilderness had cost him. All those hours of study and prayer toward one end: keeping his own will at bay, teaching himself the second-by-second discipline of self-abnegation, emptying his mind and his body of any earthly desire or need, his only joy the pure pleasure of total immersion, spiritual prostration at the feet of God. His only movement through our house was that of necessity—toward work or bathroom or bed—as though he believed that even the friction of his body through air might distract him from his quest for perfect consumption.

The silence of the rooms, the impassive eating of meals, the inert solitude, the moth-colored light—I left the house each morning, gulping air, stunned by the school-bus yellow, the lurid sky, the pale pink rise of sun. Even as my father's vision turned more and more inward, I was casting my eyes to the valley's perimeters, gauging the pull of the river, the direction a wind-loosed leaf might sail.

MAY 29, 1976: I sat in my lavender cap and gown, searching the stands for my family, some familiar face in the crowd of parents and relatives gathered to celebrate the commencement of Lewiston's senior class.

Perhaps they were there and I simply didn't see them. Or have I forgotten, having just separated myself from them so fully, having walked from my father's presence only hours before, vowing never to return?

I had wanted only to attend the supervised senior party given by the family of a classmate at their cabin 150 miles north on Coeur d'Alene Lake. My father would not give his permission, and I couldn't make sense of his denial.

"I'm eighteen," I'd said, shivering with the courage it took to question. "What if I go anyway?"

He looked at me from the brown recliner, looked at me with his cool-blue eyes, looked at me until I began to understand and not care. "Then you would have to take your things," he said, "and never come back."

I heard my mother crying in the next room. She could not defend me against her husband's wishes, could not question his authority. I did not yet know how much she feared him, how much she feared for me. When I stepped out of that house and into the blue-green ocean of May with my bag of clothes and trinkets, I breathed in the air, sweet with locust and lilac. The day walloped me with its warmth and promise of a long summer ahead. I would forget about college for a while, find an apartment, a new job. I would buy a bikini and spend Saturdays at the beach with my girlfriends, burnished brown by the sun.

I left my family's house with little regret, left my mother to her ineffectual sadness, my brother to his good boy's life. I left the church, its ridiculous rules, its warnings of evil spir-

its and perpetual damnation. I left my father to his silence. I
no longer wanted his guidance, his iron sense of direction. It
was a breach he could not bear—one, he said, he had expected all along.

The next day I traveled with my friends to Coeur d'Alene,
giddy with new freedom. I wouldn't know until later, when
my mother whispered it over the phone, that my father had
come after me, driven the long road in the dark. The lake
stretches for miles, and still my father believed he could find
me, somewhere in the hundreds of cabins and homes hidden
among the pines. I wonder now if he came with words to
mend the rift between us, or if it was anger that drove him,
made him think to push me into his car like a runaway, take
me home and keep me as he had done once before.

Had I known he was coming, I might have been afraid, sitting around the campfire, laughing with friends. But I didn't
know, and he did not find me, although he searched for
hours. It was the first time I sensed some failure in my father's ability to intuit my every move and motive. He was,
after all, only human. In his weakness, I found my strength.

For a time, I would believe that there was nothing I missed
about that home I had left. What memories I harbored were
of the earlier years spent living in the woods, when harmony
had existed between us, not of the years after—years when
the rift between my father and me had widened into an un-
crossable chasm.

Sometimes I would drive by my family's house and see
Greg putting up shots against the garage in the last light. He
was a freshman, center on the basketball team, already six
feet and still growing. He had reddish-blond hair, my

mother's fair, Germanic complexion and light blue eyes. Like her, he chose to remain silent—he brought no dishonor to the household—yet I could not bring myself to envy him. I would slow my car a little, tap the horn, and wave as though I were just passing through, a passenger aboard a train, bound for distant places.

MY FIRST APARTMENT SAT ON LEWIS-
ton's Normal Hill, where the doctors, lawyers,
and businessmen had first built their man-
sions before discovering the grander views
and higher isolation of the Snake River bluffs to the west.
The three-story house I lived in sprawled across two lots and
must have been a grand home once, before the owners
chopped its great rooms into studios for rent. Painted a
dunny avocado, it sagged with the weight of old awnings and
listing stairs.

Below the brow of the hill was downtown: the Lewis-
Clark Hotel; the Bon Marche, where my mother had hurried
me into Foundations and a training bra (the powdery sales-
woman measuring and pinching until I thought I might
faint from embarrassment); the Liberty Theater with its
stage, orchestra pit, and balcony; the Roxy, where I'd snuck to
see *Love Story* and felt the adolescent pangs of my own impending doom. Main Street, anchored to the west by the
bridge connecting Lewiston to Clarkston, Washington, ended
in East Lewiston, where the poorest and least permanent
lived, where the logging train rumbled through at midnight,
where the mill's whistle meant shift change: days to swing,

swing to graveyard, graveyard back to days. Across the Clearwater was North Lewiston, where I seldom went, where the motels charged by the hour, where the drunks stumbled out after midnight and slept in the alleys until the doors opened again.

I painted the water-stained walls of my rooms K mart white, hung a fern in the corner. Across from my bed I nailed the walnut rifle rack my great-uncle had made for me as a graduation gift, and in it I placed the Winchester 30.06 that had once belonged to my father. I had rescued it from my grandmother's closet, rubbed it free of rust, oiled its mechanism into fluid movement.

In the apartment above me I could hear the footsteps of Lonnie, a grayish man in his fifties who suffered from narcolepsy; he fell asleep over breakfast, during a shower, while rewiring the television sets he took in for repair. All night he walked, fell to the floor, woke up, and walked again. His face was bruised, his hands cut from catching on metal edges.

Across the hall from Lonnie lived Steve, a young man with Frankie Avalon hair who cut the lawn for partial rent, a job Lonnie had held until our landlady, Mrs. Stout, found him collapsed behind the mower, its blade still whirring only inches from his peacefully slumbering face.

Sometimes I found Steve outside my window or sitting on the step of my porch. When I asked what he needed, he shuffled and stammered, blushed and walked down the concrete stairs to the basement, where he folded his laundry and sometimes smoked pot. Later I would come with my Tide and bamboo basket and smell the sweet ghost of his presence.

Everyone in the building seemed to function outside normal time considerations, each passing through the halls and yard with little allegiance to sun or moon: Lonnie's nocturnal ramblings; Mrs. Stout's midnight forays to the garage, where she stashed her Jim Beam between paint cans; Steve's 2:00 A.M. serenade—"If you've got the money, honey, I've got the time." I would lie awake and imagine the loneliness of their lives, and I would feel myself alone, the pleasure of solitude slipping away.

In the practice field across the street, I could watch the Lewiston High School baseball team gather for a sabbath of spring training, cursing themselves over missed throws and fast pitches. They seemed curious to me, as did the building that rose behind them, colored pink by the early light. The past seemed impossibly distant—those times during which the halls and rooms of the school had been familiar: the sharp smell of the janitor's mop pail; the close and humid odor of lockers; the known way I traveled from one class to the next; the trophy case with its roll call of heroes. I wondered what remnant of myself I had left to what our class valedictorian had called *posterity*. National Honor Society, Thespians, Choir, German Club, editor of the literary magazine. It had seemed enough to keep me anchored in good works and moving forward into a future of successful college applications. But now that future I had imagined for myself—to become a teacher of English—was gone, replaced by my minimum-wage job as a teller at Idaho Fidelity, a ninety-five-dollar-a-month studio, a 1965 Chevrolet, Virginia Slims menthol, Boone's Farm Strawberry Hill.

So much had changed since that day only a year before, when I had left home flush with new freedom, the hours bobbing before me like fruit for the picking. At first I'd thought I might be transformed back into that girl I'd been at thirteen, who smoked and drank and let the boys who brought her drugs touch her breasts. Who hated with a loathing so pure she would have gladly given up her home, her mother and father and brother, her doting grandmother and cousins and aunts and uncles, given her soul for a chance to escape into the outside world, where dancing was not a sin, where she could listen to *Magical Mystery Tour* and wear mascara and not be cast out and down to Hell. Who had escaped for that short time, she and her dreams of California (poppies, sunshine, peace and love), only to be found and dragged back and sent away to be reborn.

I had less to prove now, less to battle against: no father to ask and answer to, no mother to frown at my clothing and hiss at the *Cosmopolitan*s I hid beneath my bed. No Sunday-morning service, no communion, no choir practice or youth group or Wednesday-evening prayer meeting. No elders telling me that the music I listened to was meant to serve Satan, no preacher predicting my damnation should I fail to heed God's word. I knew they were praying for me to see the light, to find my way back down the straight and narrow path, but I was free now, more free than I had ever been.

Yet I felt penned in, my boundaries defined by my ignorance, my uneasy acquaintance with the world. My travels had taken me to Boise, Spokane, Walla Walla. As a child, I had twice made the trip with my family to Oklahoma: once by car, missing the Yellowstone earthquake by a few hours; the second time with my mother and brother by train, relegated to our seats four endless days each way, eating from the grocery bag of peanut-butter-and-jelly sandwiches my

mother had wisely and frugally packed. My only other ramble out of Idaho had been in 1973, when my father had
driven us through one post-Christmas blizzard after another
to reach his brother's house and the monstrous wonders of
Disneyland. We'd been snowbound in Long Beach for a
week—a "freak" weather system, the forecasters pro-
claimed, that brought the city to a standstill—and I'd seen
little of the metropolis that existed outside my cousin's bedroom window.

I don't remember that I longed to experience the urban
adventures that lay beyond the Lewiston city limits, yet,
along with my friends, I complained bitterly about there
being nothing to do in the mill town we called home. A few
movie houses; a skating rink where the junior-high kids went
to smoke dope and gaze lovingly at the mirrored crystal ball;
any number of bars that wouldn't card, believing that anyone who could mouth the words "Harvey Wallbanger" was
at least the legal drinking age of nineteen. You worked at the
mill, the bullet factory, the stockyards, the Hilltop Cafe. You
were a parts runner for Napa Auto, a tire grunt for Les
Schwab. Summers you worked the peas—a backbreaking,
money-making job, twelve hours a day, seven days a week—
for as long as the annual harvest and processing of legumes
would last.

My position as a teller at Idaho Fidelity was glamorous by
comparison—$2.75 an hour, plus full benefits and two weeks
paid vacation. My friends were envious and imagined that I
would embrace job security and work my way up the teller
line, but the work dulled me: often I found myself, dollars in
hand, staring blindly past the walls of my cubicle, forgetting

my count, remembering some afternoon spent fishing Reeds Creek, wondering what insects were singing, whether the lupine had yet begun to bloom.

Like my father, whose tales of danger in the woods excited me, I believed some risks heroic and, with a good mind and strong will, most often manageable. But now, in the city, what lay out there beyond the doors of my apartment bore a definable threat. At night the old building snapped and moaned in the wind, and I jerked awake, my heart racing until I could convince myself it was not someone who had followed me home, one of the men who had seen me at the bar, where I went with girlfriends to drink sloe gin. I wore makeup and high heels; I drank and danced with men I didn't know. In the teachings of the church, this would be enough to prove my immorality: how could I expect men to remain untempted? "The kind of bait you put out," a preacher once warned, "is the kind of fish you're going to catch."

I no longer believed in any of it, not the sin or the punishment. My break from such religious doctrine had been simultaneous with my break from my father, and I'd begun to wonder what morality I possessed that had not been implanted, grafted to my soul. Having been taught that there was only one defined way to embrace spirituality, I believed that my choice was either to follow or to fall away. I could not reject part of it without rejecting the whole. "Are you *in* or are you *out?*" the preachers demanded. "Will it be Heaven, or will it be Hell?" If what it took to gain salvation was obedience to the rigid restriction of my father and the church, then I was doomed anyway. I'd dress as I wanted, do as I pleased. And then I would come home, take the Winchester from its rack, and snug it close beneath the covers, feeling its promise of safety, its hard, metallic coolness against my side.

MANY EVENINGS I spent with John, the boy I'd been dating since graduation. I had known him for several years as a classmate, but I might never have seen past his wrestler's walk, jock talk, and shyness if it hadn't been for Thane's encouragement.

Thane and John had picked me up one Saturday morning the spring of our senior year, and we'd headed for Winchester Lake for a day of fishing. This was one of the reasons I was attracted to Thane: he took me with him out of the city, back into the woods, where I could cast my line to the water, sit for hours breathing in the peppery smell of cattails and bull thistle, listening for the liquid trill of red-winged blackbirds. I would forego any number of trips to the mall for a few hours in the woods—the one place where I could feel my soul settle, where I could feel I might be home.

I'd heard stories of John's expertise as an outdoorsman, and I was eager to be part of the day's expedition. Wedged between the two boys, thigh against thigh, the new summer wind catching my hair, I'd been happy, always happy to be with Thane, though I'd come to know that, along with his girlfriend, I was only one of many who shared his affection. I'd learned this and more about Thane—how he'd lost his virginity in seventh grade, how the older girls had spoiled him silly with quickies behind the gym. I'd given up my visions of velvet evening gowns and pink corsages. Even a moment of his time seemed like a gift.

But something different came of this day. Thane had

nudged me, nodded toward John. "I should share," he whispered.

"What?" I could hardly hear him over Creedence Clearwater Revival blaring from the eight-track.

"He likes you."

For the first time I really looked at John, and what I saw enticed me: brown eyes, straight dark hair that fell across his forehead in the back rush of wind through the car. Thane moved his knee from beneath my hand, once again nodded toward John. I hesitated, then, as Thane watched, I slid my fingers up the denim seam of John's Levi's. He looked at me quickly, then at Thane, who smiled. John didn't move toward me or away, but sat there, letting me touch him, and I felt a wild exhilaration, riding between these two men, feeling their hotness and the quickness of their breathing, knowing I had this power, believing I did this not for Thane or for John but for myself: I was making my own rules, taking all that I could before the hours of my freedom ended.

And when, that May, my father had disallowed such freedom, it was John who waited for me. His mother, Viv, had taken me in like a hatchling, getting me my job at Idaho Fidelity, where she had worked for years. I'd tend my window from nine to five, counting, stacking, banding money, then come to her kitchen and watch as she tenderized roundsteak with the edge of a saucer or added a second can of mushrooms to the spaghetti sauce, smoking all the while.

Viv was a tall, dark-haired woman, once a professional model, who still credited Pond's cold cream for the fineness of her skin. I marveled at her control of fire and ash, at how elegantly she held the cigarette, elbow bent, palm up, even as she went about her domestic duties. She took her time with things, wiping the smudges from each coil of the telephone cord, peeling a carrot in smooth, considered strokes as though she were carving a child's whistle.

Walt, John's father, most often sat at the table, pushing an ashtray across the Formica with the tip of his low-tar True. He was a large, loose-jowled man given to bouts of sulking and general gruffness, a beer drinker who lightened each night around ten and spun off story after story about his days as a World War II bomber and Alaskan bush pilot. He had been my eighth-grade science teacher, and I feared he might resent that girl I had once been—smoking, cursing, setting my desk on fire with the Bunsen burner while singing Country Joe McDonald's "I-Feel-Like-I'm-Fixin'-to-Die Rag"—but in his memory my rebellion was less the sinister workings of a bad spirit than the simple boundary-testing of a teenager. I loved him for that.

Like his father, John was a man's man—a high school football star, now a running back for the university. His thighs were thicker than my waist. He had an undercut jaw and a barrel chest. Tall and lumbering, he possessed an uncommon strength, which I felt held back each time he embraced me. I loved that he was a hunter, that he knew the ravines and streams of the surrounding mountains, their secret roads and hidden meadows. I loved that he took me there, back to where I believed I could not go alone. The first time we made love was in a farmer's field, sheltered by hackberry and wild plums. I remember the warm earth beneath me, the way the magpies dipped and sculled around us, yellow pine riming the sun.

My life with John was defined by our time spent together in the outdoors. For Christmas he gave me the Ithaca 20-

gauge semiautomatic I'd seen in the window of Lolo Sporting Goods. For his birthday I bought him a Weatherby .22-250. Bolt-action, lever-action, single-shot, pump, Leupold Gold Ring 3×9 power: here was the language of my father, the numbers and names I'd heard all my life. It was all familiar to me—the rifles in the pickup's rear window, the smell of Hoppe's gun-cleaning fluid, the dank odor of downed deer, their guts pulled out in a pile, glistening and steaming, the rasp of a saw through pelvic bone as an elk was quartered and sacked to be carried. When I brought the shotgun to my cheek, the movement came to me fluid and easy—all those seasons of watching and yearning, dreaming that someday I, too, might walk the mountain and come home rich with provision.

Sometimes, after a hunt, I would stop by my parents' house, mottled with blood and feathers, still shouldering my gun, smug with success. I took a perverse pleasure in my mother's dismay. She could not understand such masculine endeavor. But it wasn't my mother I hoped to impress; it was the man who sat in his easy chair, facing the television, hardly looking my way.

My father seemed only to tolerate my presence, the few bits of speech he offered brittle and empty, hulls, husks, and chaff. From the kitchen, where I sat while my mother fried chicken in Crisco, I would ramble loudly about the shot I'd taken to bring the pheasant down, the deer I intended to hunt come October.

It was my father's land I brought back to him, I believed, his ways I embodied. The wool and flannel and denim I wore, the firearms I carried, the trails I followed. *Look at me,* I wanted to say. *Can't you see I am your daughter? Remember*

*what it was like before, when we existed together in our soli-
tude, when all that mattered was a good shot, meat on the table,
fire in the stove, a bed to share our warmth. Remember how
happy you were then. Remember what you abandoned.*

But there was no going back, no compromise. My father
had done what he believed God had asked of him, leaving
behind the only land and work he ever loved, while I had
failed in every way. It was impossible for me to be that
daughter my father had raised and taught and shaped into
being: a chaste and temperate young woman, virginal in her
marriage bed, humble before her father, her husband, her
god.

I believed it was John who might be my proxy, my way
back into my father's good grace. Over a period of several
months, I brought John with me on my visits home. My father,
though he seldom looked my way, would talk to John—
conversations about calibers and quarterbacks and carbure-
tors—and I would stand at the edge of the kitchen, where
my mother cooked. I knew I should help her with the meal,
but I couldn't resist the pull I felt when the men began their
tales of treks into the woods. I listened for what I might
learn: look for the saplings stripped by antlers, the earth
pawed clean for wallows; if you jump the deer and it runs, be
patient—the prey will sometimes circle back, curious, drawn
by its own fatal interest; always remember to mark your trail,
gauge your direction by the progress of light.

When dinner was ready, my mother, John, Greg, and I
would gather at the table while my father remained in his
chair, plate balanced on his lap. He seemed unaware of our
hushed tones, the loud emptiness that filled his place at the
head of the table, where no one else dared sit. After the meal

was over, I left as I had come, aware of my place at the margins, wondering how long my shunning would last, wondering what I could offer in place of my liberty that might make my father see me again.

Finally, there came a time when I gathered my courage and suggested that we go hunting together, my father, my brother, John, and I. I thought my father might see that I had taken up where he left off, picked up the rags of our life and pieced them back together.

That hunt took us deep into Big Bear Canyon, where I partnered up with my father, working to match his stride, to convince him he didn't have to slow down or rest for me—so little room between us for weakness, vulnerability. I wore myself out trying to keep up, denying my lesser legs and narrow shoulders, my thin wrists and ankles, believing that the race between us might never end. Without the need I felt to prove my worth, without his need to teach me worthiness, what would exist between us?

Winded, my thighs aching, I wondered at my father's stamina, his long-legged march, the hint of a hitch in his walk—the vertebrae fused solid in his lower back. He had shown me once, when I was young—the long, clean gash along his hip, from which they'd taken the shaving of bone; the larger cut that grew from the base of his spine, the skin pink and shiny as pulled taffy. When I had touched him there, pushed at the scar with my small girl's finger, I'd felt a strange and fragile resistance, the membrane of flesh so thin I feared I might hurt him, rupture the wound, cause him more pain.

Miles into our hike, we had stopped to watch a buck the color of ripe wheat cavort in a too distant field, made foolish by the doe he had followed into the open. My father smiled like some benevolent god until the deer disappeared into a tangle of hawthorn and elderberry.

"Boy, that was pretty," he'd said.

"Yes," I said. "It was." How long since I had seen that look on his face, that simple delight in the world, appreciation of something neither good nor evil, something that existed outside our realm of moral reasoning? How long since affection for anything had come unweighted by the baggage of obedience, sin, punishment, betrayal?

There would be not one hunt but several, and what I would remember is that nothing is as simple as memory. For each of our journeys into the forest, there would be a lesson I must learn: to mark my passage, to depend on no one but myself, not even my father, who walked me in, then let me lose myself and wander for hours before guiding me home.

There was no place of comfort with my father, no margin for weakness. If this was how I chose to "prove up," then my rites of passage back into my father's esteem would be on his terms, not my own. It seemed to me that nothing short of abject humility would win my father's uncompromised love. At some point, the rigors of the trial were no longer worth the little that I gained with my stoic endurance—the nearly imperceptible nods indicating his approval, the meager dole of words.

With John, it was easier. He taught me the things my father never had: how to trail whitetail and flush grouse, how to cast for rainbow and cutthroat and steelhead.

I could hardly wait for Saturdays, when John and I would sail down the highway toward the woods, through Tammany, past the 49'ers arena, the speedometer topped out and no reason to slow down. I would watch the sun slip behind the Blue Mountains, and I would remember the books I had read, the words so ripe I could taste them, and I would think, the mountains look blue because the *gloaming* has touched them; the sky is spreading its wings, feathering to *fuchsia*, *magenta*, that purple called *Tyrian*—like the colors of exotic birds, descending to a canopy of trees.

I did not speak such words aloud; no one wanted to hear them. They were fussy, temperamental. They were another of my secrets, my clandestine passions. I held them on my tongue, where they were safe. I would lay my head on John's shoulder, close my eyes, feel the muscle in his thigh tense and relax. There was another language I was perfecting, one that would seem, for a time, to take the place of all that I could not say. I spoke it to John with my mouth, my hands, my hips. At the end of the evening, he would take me home, walk me in and shut the door. We made love every night because he was a man of eighteen and I was a woman who knew little about her own desire but understood that it was the one thing she could offer that would keep him long into the night.

OUTSIDE OF JOHN, there were few friends that I spent any time with. I was uneasy in the company of women, unsure how to traverse the complex pathways of female companionship. My family's transient lifestyle had cost me the social confidence bred by lifelong friendships, and I'd consciously gone about an adherence to my father's behavior, interests, and codes—one of which, though unstated, was clear: the truest and deepest adventures can be found only in the company of men.

My cousin Les, competitive and not easily intimidated, seemed one of the few women who offered the kind of camaraderie I craved: she did not tolerate boredom. There had been years when Les and I had shared little outside of family. Even though she had often accompanied me to summer church camp, she had never fallen under the spell of fundamentalism, and during those years when I went "straight," she continued in her precocious ways, smoking, drinking, taking the punishment her parents meted out. Now, out from under our fathers' roofs, we had once again found common ground.

Les had the exotic looks of her mother—high cheekbones, bronzed skin, large, almond eyes—gifts of an Indian heritage. She worked at a clothing boutique, taking her wages in strappy dresses, gossamer negligés, four-inch heels. We spent many evenings together, downing shots of schnapps, sharing cheap wine straight from the bottle, just as we had as teenagers bent on rebellion. We smoked, we cursed the air blue, we drove to Spokane for nights of dancing, then weaved the hundred miles home, never thinking about the ways in which we endangered ourselves and others. What mattered was *staying alive*, and that had little to do with physical survival. Our greatest fear was inertia, of finding ourselves gone still while the world revolved on around us.

It was with John and the other young men who shared his love of the outdoors that I found my truest fraternity. They took me in, allowed me to exist in that strange place between one of the guys and a girl to be protected. My favorite was Brock Hoskins, a shy Catholic boy with fine brown hair and chestnut eyes. He had a gentleness about him, quiet ways, and I often found him watching me. He leaned across the pickup seat one time, whispered in my ear, "John is a damn lucky guy to have you." The sentiment—so sweet and old-fashioned—made me girlish, and I blushed.

Whenever we dropped Brock off at his parents' house, his passel of younger brothers and sisters came to the door, and he was embarrassed but happy. I'd wave to his mother, a tall, round woman, good in her Catholic ways, who came to the window and smiled, wiping her hands on a dish towel. I wondered at her life—so many children, so little outside of house and family. I could not imagine forever being left behind, incarcerated with Comet and Pine-Sol, waiting for the men to return from their work, their fields and pastures, their games, their fishing trips and hunting camps. Always, the women waiting, waiting like my mother had for my father to come home unscarred and upright from the woods. Instead, he came home cut and bruised and finally broken, flat on his back in a body cast for a year while she worked at the café to support us.

Left behind: nothing scared me more. Perhaps a remnant of my fundamentalist faith, believing that God would return at any moment to take his chosen ones home. Or maybe it was the loneliness and boredom I feared, the sense of panic that swelled in my chest when the rooms grew quiet and I was left without distraction.

And so I followed John everywhere: to the tip of Hoover Point, to the bottom of the Salmon River canyon. When John and Brock took up motocross, I bought my own dirt bike and rode behind them on rutted raceways and logging roads. We roared across pastureland, meadows, and creek beds, along trails too narrow for one, dodging wind-felled snags and sawn-off stumps. I came to believe that my fear was what fu-

eled me, and that as a woman I had never been allowed to
call it by any other name—a rush, a dangerous thrill, a jolt of
excitement and daring. The landscape was a blur of spruce
and tamarack, sumac and dog fennel. I loved the way it all
flew by, the way I could speed through hours and eat nothing
but air. When we rested, we eyed each other with a kind of
pleasure, flushed with adrenaline, sensuous in our damp
skins and panting. Then John would move closer to me,
Brock would take his eyes to the breaks of the canyon, the
horizon clouded by harvest, and we would sit that way, content in our place, catching our breath, once again on familiar
ground.

I REMEMBER the summer afternoon I stood with Viv in the
kitchen, spreading deviled ham across slices of Wonder
bread. John and I planned to pick up Brock and drive several
hours south, across the prairie, down Eagle Creek to the
Salmon, the River of No Return. John had loaded the motor-
cycles, rifles, and fishing rods. We'd make a day of it, maybe
even spend the night, throw our bags on the sand where the
canyon walls echoed the rise and roll of sturgeon.

As I filled the cooler, I heard the wail of an ambulance,
distant, then close, then trailing off. The shrillness of the
siren faded. The phone rang. Walt grunted into the receiver,
listened, looked from beneath his eyebrows at the rest of us,
circled around him and frozen by the sudden slackness of his
face.

"Ah, sweet Jesus," he said, then handed the phone to John.

By the time we got to the hospital, the doctors and nurses
had cut Brock out of his Levi's and T-shirt, started IV's, in-

serted a catheter, shaved his head and wrapped it in layers of gauze. Several of Brock's brothers and sisters sat outside his room, the younger ones concentrating hard on the pictures they drew, the older ones tearful, arms crossed, holding themselves. The father, a carpenter and rancher, hadn't yet been reached. Brock's mother turned toward us and gripped John's arm.

"He was just going for a ride until you got there. Just a short ride down the road." She looked into my face, searching for some reason why such an easy story had broken down.

I looked past her, through the windows of Intensive Care, where the medical personnel, who never assume a story's ending, clustered at the railings of Brock's bed. One came toward us, nodded.

"Are these the friends?"

There was an ominous tone to his voice, accusatory and defining, as though we were somehow responsible. I looked at the man's hands and arms—cuticles scrubbed into nonexistence, the dark hair on his knuckles and wrists at odds with the sterility of his skin.

"Do you understand he probably can't hear you? Don't try to shake or startle him. There's no response at this time, but he might—" He stopped, considered the mother's face, how she had caught the word *might* and how he mustn't be responsible for instilling hope. "Sometimes, not very often but it's not unheard of, it's not impossible that he could conceivably respond to your voice. We've seen it in these cases. The comatose patient is unpredictable. You'll have five minutes."

Comatose. I mulled the word as John and I followed the man into the dark room. Iridescent lines and numbers radiated from the monitor screens. A nurse leaned into the light of the observation window, checking her clipboard notes.

Brock was on his back, sleeping, it seemed, except for the tubes and bandages and dried smears of blood across his jaw and throat. He wore no gown, just the hospital sheet stamped ST. JOSEPH. Down the hall a woman howled, in pain or rage, I couldn't tell which.

I smoothed the sheet, realized as I took in this man, whom I had known before he was a man, that even in the heat of hard rides and late summer hunts I had never seen his bare chest. He was modest, like my father, who would never think to strip below his undershirt in front of a woman not his wife.

I leaned over Brock, smelled the sharp blood odor of his breath. If I had been alone, I might have touched him there, where the twin wings of his rib cage met, touched with one finger the softness that rose and fell with the delicate pulse of a newborn's skull. I slid my fingers beneath Brock's hand, felt the cold, talcum smoothness of his palm. What was it about hospitals that forced everyone's temperature to the level of just-cooled wax? I looked at the monitors. Nothing quickened. Nothing slowed.

The green-suited man stepped in, moved to the bed. He pulled Brock's right eyelid back, pointed a thin flashlight at the pupil, let the lid drop, made notes on the clipboard. Outside the door, Brock's mother stood waiting.

"Did he move? Anything?" I shook my head. She slumped back in her chair. "Three days, they say. After that, there's not much to hope for."

I wanted to tell her what I once knew of faith. Hadn't I believed that my hands held the power to draw from the sick their disease, that I could raise a cripple from his bed? I thought of those meetings, the need I had felt to move toward one believer or another and say to him, to her, "I feel what you feel—the pain is *here*," then cup the ear pulsing with infection, the spastic back. Whatever part of me throbbed or ached or twitched with injury was mirrored in the body before me. *Touch, pray, believe*. The pain would sharpen, then fade.

Something had worked in me then. In the months to come, I would stand beside Brock's bed, hold his fingers like the delicate offering of a maiden, close my eyes and remember the heat that had come to my hands. But I could not pray for him. The words were no longer mine.

THE DOCTORS MOVED BROCK from one hospital to another, then, finally, his family brought him home. Although his eyes were open, he focused on nothing. His body made its own demands: his arms twitched, his fingers jerked to satisfy an itch. He groaned loudly and smacked his lips. His body went rigid with the urge to defecate. Each day it was the same: the sight and smell of a nineteen-year-old body gone back to its child's ways. No matter how attentive his mother, some puréed food remained to be tongued and pushed from the corners of his mouth. He sweated the sweat of a man against the plastic beneath his bedding. His urine flowed strong and yellow through the catheter and into the bag. When he belched, mucus fluttered in his throat.

I see it as a turning point now—that time after Brock's accident, when John struggled to balance his studies with the demands of football, when he became more and more bitter. He quarreled with his parents; more often than not, he spent his nights with me. As though punishing themselves for their own continued existence, John and the other young men who were left began to fight, first with rivals in the parking lots of bars, and then with each other. My last memories of our small tribe together involve scenes of drunken brawling, the girlfriends fretful and pleading from the sidelines.

And still we danced, to whatever music came down to us from the band or the deejay, on the dance floor or in fields mown down by last harvest, the pickup doors thrown wide and every radio tuned to KRLC, the keg on the side and fire in the middle, our shadows tying us to the black shroud of sky.

Those seem impossible hours when we threw ourselves, drunk and reeling, into the morning. Perhaps it is because of what has happened since to so many of our number—violent death, alcoholism, grief-stricken marriages, and lost children—that I see those last weeks with John as dark and foreboding. Or maybe it's because I now know what my own future held that I remember the days closing down around me, the nights longer, swallowing the light.

I would not know it then, but John would have given me all that he could, and I would have taken all that he could offer. Over the next several months, what held between us began to unravel, and we lost the tenderness we once shared—the way he came to me after hours on the playing field, how I kissed his thighs, his ribs, the bruises so deep they rose like oil from the bone. I didn't realize that I was beginning another journey, a journey that would take me even farther away from my father, my family, away from all that had once sustained me. I didn't know that over the next two years I would lose myself in a wilderness so dark and foreign that no one could find me. For a time, I would believe that there was no road back, and I would exist that way: my eyes closed, my hands fisted, unable to see, unable to remember the secrets of my passage. I would lie beneath blankets and shiver with cold, dreaming the coyotes outside my window, dreaming the river, dreaming a deer gone silent in its bed, hidden in spring fern and hemlock, holding still, so still the ravens gave up their vigil, took flight from the branches, and disappeared, black stars in the bluest sky.

"YOU'VE GOT TO DRIVE TO WORK A different way each day."

Mr. Hampton, the large, ruddy-faced president of Idaho Fidelity, held up a map of the city, its main arteries highlighted in red, little arrows pointing to the heart of our building. "Keep a schedule in your car so you know which way you've come. Take a different street home. Don't take that route again for a couple of days."

The tellers, secretaries, loan officers, and janitor sat in a half circle. The janitor was taking notes.

We'd been notified the day before that a 7:30 A.M. meeting had been called. I'd groaned, already dreading the lost half hour of sleep. All these precautions seemed nonsense, anyway, motivated by the kidnapping, botched ransom, and death of a banker's daughter somewhere in the East. Lenders across the country had decided that anyone connected to financial institutions—family, tellers, janitors—was at risk of being nabbed and held for millions of dollars.

I yawned, recrossed my legs, listened to the *scritch* of the janitor's pencil. Friday was a painful prelude to Saturday, when I could sleep until noon and not be bothered by rules and directives. I half hoped that John might stop by, but he came to me less often now. We had agreed that we were too young to be so serious. Part of me realized that I was better off without him, that he was no longer the well-mannered high school boy with whom I had fallen in love. His perpetual drunkenness was a kind of self-destruction I didn't understand, and when he came to me late at night, bloodied from yet another parking-lot fight, I scolded him while dabbing at his wounds with a peroxide-soaked rag.

"Kim, are you listening?" Mr. Paul, our vice president, was demonstrating the silent alarm. I straightened in my chair and nodded, wishing that some thug would abduct the skinny man with his Vandyke beard and manicured nails.

Despite the bank's insistence, I drove home from work that afternoon the same way I had come. My apartment was only eight blocks away, and it seemed silly to zigzag through the neighborhood like a lost tourist. I was tired of the rules, the sour face of Mr. Paul. I wanted to get away from the parking lots soaking up heat, sticky beneath my heels, away from the businessmen in their ridiculous suits, who eyed me over their fives and twenties, who touched my wrists with their pale dry hands.

"YOU WANT TO HAVE YOUR CAKE and eat it too," my mother scolded whenever I complained about the boredom of my job, my dissatisfaction with the men I dated. What *did* I want? Most often, the answers came to me in the negative: I wanted *not* to have my mother's life, defined by domestic service and silence. I wanted *not* to be bound by fear of a man's displeasure, his anger and strength. I did not want to need a man to make me feel safe. What I longed for was someone with whom I might share all the sides of myself, someone who could teach me both the signs of animals and the language of man. I wanted to lie beneath stars in a meadow ringed by cedar, have my lover whisper to me the names of distant constellations.

But who? The fraternity boys bored me with their beer-guzzling games and hands brushing my breasts. The cowboys took me to the Villa for biscuits and gravy at midnight, ate without a word, then chaperoned me back to my doorstep, where they thumbed out their chew and waited politely to be asked in. The church boys had shied away long ago, although I would sometimes catch them driving by after Sunday-evening service, cruising my apartment as though they might catch a note of something decadent, calling to them like a siren's song.

"But you *need* a man," my mother insisted, and I believed that she thought any man was better than none. The idea of living alone horrified her; if her husband were to leave, she would become prey, made vulnerable by her inability to keep her man clean and content. She and my father had this un-derstanding between them—that with her attendance to his needs, she bought herself both shelter and shield.

If such were the case, I'd do without, I said. I had my guns and my knives. I was taking karate, "the way of the empty hand." I'd have my brown belt by fall.

My mother sighed, shook her head. This was a rebellion of a different kind, one she believed no less dangerous than my early flight from home. I was defying my nature, refusing my role. When would I stop wanting to act like a man, stop wanting to *be* one? I wanted too much, always, too much.

I was waiting, for what I wasn't sure. It was more than the

reliability of a biweekly paycheck, the sound of John's Chevy pulling into the driveway, the voices of friends coming to pick me up and take me to the bar. It was something else, distant and unnameable. It was in the light that turned the dry hills to the north the colors of gemstones: amethyst and topaz, jasper and jade. It was in the slight wind that came off the river and up the valley, bringing with it the smells of sage and locust and something of the sea. I would sit on my kitchen counter, bare feet in the sink, smoking, pressing my lips lightly against the window screen, tasting the dust and warm rain, my breath sieving through wire, rising, disappearing into the shadows of sycamore, and I would study the air, feeling as though I were the eye at the hurricane's center, bedeviled by calm, unable to move as the world spun away around me. When all that was left for me to see was my own dark reflection in the glass, I would make my way to bed, where I could prop myself against the headboard and read until dawn.

I read the story of the Scottsboro Boys, wrongfully accused of raping a white woman. I read *Portnoy's Complaint* and *Catch-22* and *Fear of Flying*, interspersed with thin tales of tortured romance: the soldier who desired a princess, the countess who desired a sailor, the sailor who loved the plantation owner's daughter, the daughter who lusted for her father's prize slave—the story always the same, less graphic and vulgar than the books I'd found in my uncle's room, but the same. Always the woman at first refusing, the man wanting and pursuing, then, too many times rebuffed, turning away, so that she must somehow win back his favor. I was drawn to the mysteriously charged eroticism produced by such battles of wills—how badly we want what we cannot have, how we savor the struggle, how the prize is so much sweeter when harder won.

Yet I hated the games I felt forced to play, the luring of men and then the denial. Perhaps my mother was right— maybe there *was* something male in me. I wanted to be both pursuer and pursued, dominate and submissive, predator and prey. At times my fantasies were romantic gambols, breathless near-unions, heartbreaking separations, the desperate anticipation of release. Other times my dreams took a turn that I could only interpret as dark: I was the one directing and demanding, the one whose strength could overwhelm, the one who could force compliance.

During those hours alone, when I allowed my mind to follow its fancy, I came to the deepening belief that there was something freakish in my nature, something dangerous and destructive. I could not imagine speaking of my fantasies to John, who believed that sex suited men but who was made uncomfortable by a woman's taking undue interest in the practice. Some nights, when John was not with me, I found contentment in the Harlequin paperbacks; other nights I waited until the traffic had left the streets, then made my way to the twenty-four-hour quick mart, where I bought the adult magazines and books that promised something more graphic than rippling biceps and heaving bosoms. I blushed beneath the knowing eye of the midnight clerk, who took his time bagging my purchases. Back at my apartment, I could lock the doors, draw the blankets close, and be alone with my saturnalia of words.

Books and passion—the two became inseparable, and

what fed one fed the other. There was a kind of desperation I felt, as though there would never be enough time for both, as though I couldn't read and learn and know fast enough to feed the engine of my mind and body. I wanted more *now;* I needed to know *now.* Such appetite could be cultured and trained like a gentlewoman's topiary, or it could run wild, grow rampant and rapacious—it could swallow me whole. My father had recognized and directed my ravening curiosity. Out from under his husbanding eye, I felt the vines twining, kudzu and bamboo, the ground growing feral beneath my feet.

I WAS COUNTING the final minutes until closing when the red Corvette Stingray pulled up at the bank's drive-through window. That first time I noticed only the car, the man's long fingers and shaggy black hair, his eyes, which were crazy blue. He was not handsome—a large nose, a pronounced Adam's apple beneath the nest of his beard. When I counted his money, I did not have to look up to know that he was watching my face instead of my hands.

And that's what I remember most, the way he *watched* me. I was not yet twenty. My long brown hair was layered and curled, my fingernails polished, my makeup carefully applied to bring out the blue of my own eyes. I might have expected a man to look at me, perhaps even allow his glance to linger. But this was different. The man in the 'Vette settled into his gaze as though it humored him to do so.

I thumbed out the bills for him, counting by twenties, slid the metal box from my closet of bulletproof glass. When he asked my name, I told him, and he smiled. I remember the smallness of his teeth, his ease. Even with other cars lined up behind him, he took his time slipping the money into his wallet, lighting his cigarette. He seemed to swallow the smoke, letting a thin line of it escape each nostril before raising an eyebrow my way.

I watched him pull into traffic, checked my watch. Friday with its long lines and mill paychecks seemed never to end. A few more minutes and I could lower the shade that read SORRY, WE'RE CLOSED and be gone for the weekend.

Please let me balance tonight, I thought. One nickel off and we'd all have to stay, six women at six windows, counting and recounting. The *girls,* they called us. We were mostly loyal to the bank, more so to one another. No one complained if another didn't balance. Everyone stayed, checking the debits and credits, lighting up a cigarette because the bank was closed and the customers were gone. It looks bad, we were told, for a woman to smoke in public. The men could smoke at their desks—Mr. Paul, Mr. Hampton, who ushered customers from his office to our windows with a sweep of his Salem.

It was Mr. Paul we answered to, and I believed he hated us all, perhaps women in general but especially me, the youngest of the tellers. I had broken all the rules of the bank at least once, and now I was breaking another: no chewing gum while on the teller line. Bent over my work, I was startled by Mr. Paul's hand appearing beneath my chin. I dutifully spat the gum into his palm. His nostrils flared in distaste as he carried the wad to the wastebasket, turned his hand over, and dropped it in. The customers watched him, then looked at me. I shrugged, embarrassed like a child is embarrassed, shamed, and stricken with helpless anger. People shuffled, coughed. I began my count over.

"HE'S A DICK," Charlene said later, lifting her chin and blowing smoke toward the ceiling.

I nodded, glad to be balanced and out of the bank, at the bar with Charlene drinking daiquiris. Charlene was New Accounts, moved up from teller because her line was always longest. She had a way with people. She had red hair, green eyes, a Barbie-doll figure, a smile that meant something. I loved seeing her change out of skirts, nylons, and high heels into the tight Wranglers and manured boots of a weekend rancher. She was twenty years older than I was, and I was both puzzled and pleased by her attention.

Tony, Charlene's boyfriend, had shown up at the bank that afternoon on his way out of town, catching the door just at closing, just as Mr. Hampton slid his key into the inside lock. Everyone had watched as Tony strolled across the lobby to Charlene's desk. He wasn't tall, but he was solid and probably a little mean the way cowboys can be. He'd leaned toward her and smiled, then slid out his tongue, a quarter balanced on its tip.

I thought I might be a little in love with Tony myself. If I told Charlene, I knew what she would say: "You think you can handle him, honey, you go right ahead." I wanted to be like that: in control but with an edge. I could never find that fine line between the bad girl and the good, and right then I felt like a failed audition for both.

Charlene and I smoked together, filling our ashtray with her lipstick-kissed Winstons and my Virginia Slims.

"Tell me what you're thinking," Charlene said.

I stubbed out one cigarette and lit another, as I'd learned to do when the talk turned serious. "I don't know. How men are."

Charlene laughed. She believed in keeping her men guessing. "Got to give them a little, but not too much," she'd say, and even though I knew some women were capable of such magic, I also knew that I wasn't one of them. I was no good at the games, the push and pull, the approach and retreat.

"When Tony gets home," Charlene said, "he's going to fill me so full. . . ." She gave a tight moan and closed her eyes. Then she began to laugh, that deep, rolling laugh that anyone could see was honest, and pretty soon we were both laughing, slumped sideways in the booth, the men at the bar grinning, shaking their heads, and the bartender saying, "Somebody better buy those ladies a drink."

We drank until there was no rum left, then stumbled into the night, rummaging through our purses for keys. I made it home and into my bathroom before getting sick. I clung to the porcelain, intent on keeping the walls still long enough so I could fall asleep or pass out or do whatever it took to stop the roiling deep in my gut.

I wiped my mouth, blew my nose, looked at myself in the mirror. Strands of hair stuck to the sides of my face. Mascara and eye shadow smeared my temples; spittle shone on my chin. I didn't care. Who was I afraid might see me, anyway?

I slipped to the floor, rested on the green throw rug my mother had given me, then covered myself with a towel, still damp from that morning's bath. Knees drawn tight against my chest, I shivered beneath the white brilliance of the two bare bulbs on either side of the mirror, wishing for 7-Up and saltines, my mother's cure for stomachache. I longed for her cool hand, her voice telling me I'd feel better soon. I thought of her lying in bed next to my father, and I felt a sharp pang of loneliness. When either of them was ill, the other was always there, bringing bowls of Campbell's soup, offering toast and sweet tea. How much was it worth to have such a companion, someone to care for you, someone to brush the hair from your forehead?

I thought about the guy in the 'Vette. He was not my *type*, not jockish or boy-next-door cute, yet I felt drawn to him for reasons I could not name. Years later, I would meet women who would have wanted him immediately, women whose dreamed-of lovers bore the deep marks of hard living, dangerous to the core. I'd told Charlene that there was something about him that intrigued me. It wasn't just the car or his attention. Something I sensed more than saw, a kind of familiar intimacy. He made me feel funny, like he knew something about me, like there was this *secret*.

At the bar, I'd whispered to Charlene what I had gleaned from his deposit slip and account information: his name was David M. Jenkins. He lived at 542 Meadowlark Lane, Apartment C. I knew that he had $3,987.55 in checking and over $1,000 in savings, which seemed like a lot of money to me. I knew his paychecks came out of Oregon and that he was much older than I was.

What I didn't know was that he was a long-haul truck driver with a speed habit and an envelope full of Quaaludes, that he knew more about guns, traps, and pelts than any man

I had ever met, that he had a great horned owl mounted on his wall and a pistol under his pillow. That the Corvette was not his, and that what he knew about me had nothing to do with money or age and everything to do with the hunt: he had chosen me. He was waiting, watching me more carefully than I could ever imagine.

WHEN THE FLOWERS CAME—A DOZEN long-stemmed red roses spraying their scent into the bank's lobby—Mr. Paul could barely contain his distaste. When customers asked who the flowers were from, I said, "David," as though his name were already familiar and expected.

I took the roses home and set them on the small dinette. Their color, gaudy and warm, brightened the room. Several days later the Corvette was back at my window.

"Do you like steak and lobster?"

I nodded at David from my post at the drive-through, trying to remember if I had ever eaten lobster.

"Tuesday night?"

"I have karate lessons on Tuesdays and Thursdays."

David raised an eyebrow. "Black belt yet?"

"Not yet." I wished that he would take my cue and lower his voice, which boomed from the single speaker. Mr. Paul had noticed the length and probable inappropriateness of our conversation and was craning his neck my way. I pushed the drawer further out.

"Wednesday?" he asked. Smoke from his cigarette wafted into the bin.

"Sure. Okay." I scribbled my address on a debit slip and pushed it against the window for him to read. He did not bother to write it down, and I wondered how he would remember it.

"See you at seven." He winked, then motored casually out of the lot. I turned to see the entire line of tellers staring at me. I shrugged, grinning, until Mr. Paul clapped his hands twice, sending us all back to our ten-keys.

FROM MY KITCHEN WINDOW I watched the Corvette pull into the driveway, saw David step from the car and straighten. His height startled me. I was used to tall men— John, my father, my uncles and brother all over six feet—but not to David, who beat them by several inches, whose wrists and ankles showed long and lean beyond his cuffs. "Built for speed, not comfort," he joked, and I liked that he could laugh at himself.

He opened the Corvette's passenger door, which swung out wide and low. He kept his window cracked enough to draw out the smoke. He didn't gun the car across the bridge but steered it smoothly through traffic, content with his control. As we talked I studied the hard angles of his face, the thin length of his legs. He was nothing like John. I liked his full, eye-wrinkling smile, the roughness of his skin—proof that he'd seen some things, knew what mattered.

Cedars III was as plush as restaurants got in the valley— red carpet, heavy drapes, more silverware than I knew what to do with. Miniature loaves of dark bread came on little wooden boards. I remembered the first time I had been in the restaurant: prom night with John, who had thought the small brown loaf a potato and reprimanded the waitress for bringing him a spud he hadn't ordered. I rolled my eyes at the memory.

"What are you thinking?" David asked.

"Nothing, really. Do you come here a lot?"

He grinned. "Haven't been, but I think I will."

He might have said more, reached across the white linen tablecloth and touched my hand, but he didn't. He left it that way, a hint of expectation. Instead, we began to get acquainted, and soon our talk turned toward an interest we shared: the woods and the ways of the hunt.

He seemed delighted by my knowledge of the outdoors. He listened and agreed or disagreed, and then we fell into jocular argumentation about whitetail versus muleys, bolt-action versus pump.

When David told me about his work, the semi-truck he drove from Lewiston to Seattle one night, then back the next, with a few days off between trips, I was again reminded of my father. But there was a difference: I noted the dark circles beneath David's eyes, the eyes themselves shot through with red. His shirt was wrinkled; he needed a haircut. My mother would have seen it immediately: he had no woman at home.

We ate the thick tenderloins rare, the way he said they needed to be. The lobster tail we dipped in little pots of melted butter, kept warm over candles. I loved it, loved the way the flesh melted on my tongue. It was white, firm, *succulent*, I thought, and looked up to find David watching me, leaned back and smiling. I saw then what the evening might cost.

But I was wrong. That night David walked me to my door, told me how much he'd enjoyed my company, then turned away without a touch. I watched him pull out of the driveway and disappear around the corner. I was surprised and relieved but also concerned. In my experience with men, satisfaction with my presence had always expressed itself in the physical: if the night had gone well, the man would at least attempt some contact, and I would have the choice of demurring or acquiescing. David's simple exit had left me feeling empty, unsettled, as though the play had ended without its final scene.

Inside my apartment, I flipped on the TV, then turned it off. I paced the length of the small rooms. I ran a bath, covered my face with the steaming washrag. I wondered if he would call me again.

THURSDAY EVENING I pulled on my stiff white *gia* and knotted the sash showing my rank in the martial art of Do Shin Kan. It made me feel stronger to learn the kicks and parries, but it was the *kata* I most enjoyed—geometric dance, the grace and force of contained movement, the wide arcs and small circles our feet and fists made through air. The sparring I liked least, always a little afraid of the men I fought, whose height and weight made me desperate to kick and run. I came home bruised—my forearms from blocking, my sides from blows I should have deflected. The skin of my knuckles broke and scarred from hours spent boxing a tape-wrapped plank. Even the rubber-bladed knives with which we mimed battle caught me with their spurred edges, scratching more than cutting—long, shallow wounds that stained my *gia* with blood.

I loved the discipline, the will it took, the concentration,

the denial of pain, and I loved the mysticism—the medita-
tion a kind of prayer. In the gym with the lights off, the glow
of the streetlamps shut out by the heavy, industrial shades,
we sparred blind.

"Listen," our sensei would whisper, "and you will hear the
muscle tense, you will feel the passage a sleeve makes
through air."

Afterward we sat cross-legged on the floor, concentrating
on the dark. "You must find a place to go to, where your mind
can be soothed, where the wind is a comfort, the water tran-
quil, the air warm and sweet." I closed my eyes and went
back to the woods, to the meadow and stream, the breeze
spiced with camas.

"Breathe with your stomach," the sensei said. He touched
me where my rib cage ended and the softness of my belly
began. "Here," he said, and I made my muscles tighten
against his hand.

I pulled the air in, pushed the air out, until my pulse
slowed and the blood that rushed through my ears was the
brush of pine against pine, the sound the caddis made when
I was ten and the day held still so that I might listen, my
head laid back and resting in grass, the grass so high that no
one could see me there, a girl stretching lean to welcome the
sun.

My guns, my knives, my feet and fists—I thought I might
keep myself safe. Had I forgotten the books, the stories I had
learned? The fruit of the tree, ripe and unblemished, the
snake. Leda beneath a summer sky, its clouds gathering low
like swan's wings. The spring's new flowers, the ones
Persephone pulled from the earth, meaning only to breathe
in their sweetness. I had forgotten that things are not always

as they seem—that what catches you can come in light, bearing no weapons, open, alluring, calling your name.

DAVID DECIDED our next date would be to the woods. I could hardly wait to feel the cool canopy of trees, to walk the hills where bear had clawed through heart-rotted cedar in search of grubs. He picked me up in a new four-wheel-drive Ford with a matching canopy, an eight-thousand-pound Warn winch on the bumper: he was prepared for the rutted roads, the deep pockets of mud left by spring thaw. I handed him the Ithaca shotgun John had bought me for Christmas—the stock with its lovely grain, the breech so finely engraved—and felt a moment's regret. But its worth to me now had to do not with John but with David, who admired the gun but didn't ask how I came to have it. There was very little he asked, and his willingness to keep our attention on the present comforted me: my teenage romances had begun to seem juvenile and embarrassing. I wanted this older man to see me as mature, a worthwhile companion.

We drove south along the edge of the Nez Perce Indian Reservation, climbing toward the summit of Winchester Grade, onto the Camas Prairie. From the high flats the land looks unbroken; only when we reached the lip of the wide, millennial cuts could we see the abrupt drop-off of long-worked fields into basalt canyons, miles of hidden draws, home to whitetail and bobcat. But it was spring, and other than a few magpies rowing through the air with their black-and-white wings, we had little on which to aim our guns. We stood at the edge of a meadow near the crossroads settlement of Melrose, and I followed David's lead, blowing the early monarchs and lacewings into velvet tatters. I remember being made uneasy by such casual cruelty, but I dared not protest. Just as when I'd watched John sight in the starlings and inky ravens, I knew that any emotional response on my part would compromise the place I held in the company of men.

As we drove the gravel roads, David told me he had been raised in Lewiston. Some of his family lived up north, where the best hunting could be found: deer, elk, bear, grouse, moose if you drew a tag. He said he hunted coyotes to bring in extra money, that he hoped the coming winter would be as the *Farmer's Almanac* had promised: long and hard. Cold more than anything brought on the best pelts. Maybe, he said, he'd take me with him.

I'd done my share of varmint shooting from roadsides and pickup windows, even as I secretly longed to let the coyotes be. I admired their efficiency, the way they multiplied and prospered despite the ranchers' poisons. I loved the way they materialized from roadside brush, the way they loped across the sage and rocks, especially the way their single voices rose together in mezzosoprano yips, raucous and joyful and pleased with the moon. Still, I said yes, I would go with him and learn how to fashion a blind of snow and branches, how to wrap my rifle in a torn white sheet, how to blend into the landscape and make the sounds of wounded prey and wait for the coyotes to come.

We talked of range and trajectory, camouflage and blinds. But if David was impressed with my woodsman's knowledge, he didn't say so but simply nodded, as my father might. There was, in fact, much about him to remind me of my father. He smoked with the same casual intensity, had about him the same air of self-possession, the kind of near-arrogance backed with quietude that seems to suggest strength. Physically, he was taller, thinner, and not nearly so handsome. But their eyes were the same—clear, sapphire blue.

David, like my father, was a curious, engaged observer of the world. He'd read many of the same books on supernatural phenomena that I had, and he added to his firsthand knowledge of the ways of animals by referring to his extensive library of texts on the habits of prey, tanning techniques, big-game tales. He spent a great deal of time contemplating possibility, applying his analytical mind to various problems and projects. During the long drives across the mountains and flatlands of northern Idaho, David and I would take turns debunking each other's theories on creation, evolution, ESP, extraterrestrial life.

Did I tell David about the miracles of my past, how I had once felt the rush of heat in my hands as I prayed for the sick, how I'd spoken in tongues and believed in the guidance of angels? Did we talk of God, Heaven, the Hell we might burn in? If so, I don't remember, but I remember instead the games we played, badgering each other's logic, challenging proof. And I think of how I've always been eager for a round of debate, how, as a girl, it was then that I felt my father's greatest approval—when the gifts of good grades and exemplary behavior, even the gift of my child's embrace, were not enough. What my father wanted from me were my moments of intellectual awareness, when he could see the workings of my mind. "Think," he would say, his eyes narrowing. It was not a directive but a command. "You go *think*." Only when I had come to a logical insight or conclusion would I come back, and then there would be the reward of his smile.

Over the next several weeks, as David and I spent more and more time together, I told him about my father, our alienation. I told him about John, how everything had changed after Brock's accident. What little David told me of his life came in bits: he'd been married for a short while to a woman with three children; his mother and younger sisters still lived in Lewiston, in the house where he had been raised; his father had left the family years before. It had been up to him to provide, to bring home the seasonal kill to keep the long months' hunger at bay.

David knew the old homesteads where trees still bore the dwarfish fruit whose sweet decay brought deer to feed. He could project and intersect the lope of a spooked whitetail, decide if and when a buck would come back to its favored thrashing tree. I marveled at the practiced way he moved through the rough hedges of hackberry, the way his mouth dropped open to listen for the snap of a twig, the brush of a flank against pine.

When he told me that the Corvette had been borrowed from a friend, I didn't care; I was coming to like him much better behind the wheel of his own Ford four-wheel-drive. He took me deeper into the mountains, along the breaks of the Salmon and the Snake. I packed bologna sandwiches, and we ate them sitting on the pickup's tailgate, looking out over Idaho to the Wallowa Range of Oregon. It was there, open to miles and miles of wilderness, that David gave me one of the few stories I would ever hear him tell—how, as a teenager, he had traveled with two schoolmates over the same rutted roads, scanning the hillsides for game. The boy in the middle, afraid to pass up a close kill, had kept his rifle in hand, balanced between his knees, barrel pointed upward.

David recalled the deafening noise of the discharge but not stopping the pickup, only that he opened the door and fell to the ground, wounded and bleeding. He understood first that the rifle had gone off, then that the blood that covered his face and arms was both his and not his: the bullet had entered under the other boy's chin, sending out shards of bone.

I imagined the one slumped forward against the pickup's dash, his face gone. Miles from a phone and no choice but for the two left alive to crawl back in beside their friend. I didn't ask how it felt to do that—spattered with bits of cartilage and brain, trying to remember the familiar road that would lead them out of the forest.

I felt a new intimacy with David, as though in giving me this story he was allowing me closer to his heart. That boy who had steered the gory hearse home was now the man who taught me to trail in thick cover and listen for the language of birds, who knew the woods as a hermit might, instinctively drawn to the shadows where grouse imagined themselves safe. And that girl who had chased the grouse from their secret places and shot them with BB's was now a woman seeking a companion, wanting a man who loved what she loved, knew what she needed to know—a man who could find his way into the woods and live there, be happy there, and stay.

WHEN NOT IN THE MOUNTAINS, David and I went to movies, dined on steak and lobster, had drinks at the bars, where my friends saw me and waved. At first I was embarrassed by David's gangly, disheveled appearance and by his age, but then I began to feel protective of him. They didn't know how lovely it was to carry on a conversation about something other than spectacular drunks and fraternity shenanigans. I found myself laughing more, happy to be free of the foolishness of boys.

Still, I felt I barely knew this man with whom I was beginning to spend every available hour. His desire to be with me was clear. Why, then, hadn't we moved beyond a simple kiss? The dance of desire I'd braced myself for never happened—not even the first step. David had kept himself from me, intentionally so, not without interest but with absolute control. I wondered if he was afraid, doing this out of old-fashioned respect or some kind of weird hang-up. I had wondered initially if he might be gay, but his attention, even from a distance, was recognizably voracious—something I could almost smell rather than see. Whatever it was, I'd gotten used to it, even comfortable, able for the first time to be alone with a man without worrying that he'd jump me the minute the pleasantries were over. I felt relief from the burden of decision, from the guilt of having given in or having said no, from disappointment and rejection. It was an incredible freedom, one I hadn't felt since my girlhood, since before that first boy, the preacher's son, had touched my knee in the parsonage's dark stairway, whispered in my ear, cleaved me in two with his words of want.

As David's celibacy continued, my initial relief grew into an intense curiosity, a hunger I had never felt for John or any other lover. It was not simply sexual; it was intellectual as well. It was a yearning I didn't recognize but David did—a hunter trained to patience, knowing everything with his eyes.

WHEN DAVID FIRST TOOK ME to meet his mother, I believed that I might finally know something more about him than what I'd been able to glean from his stunted narratives. What I found was a strong-boned woman with black hair to her shoulders, a hard smoker, kind but quiet in my presence. The house she and her teenage daughters shared sat at the front of a large lot, sole holdout against the rapid commercialization that surrounded them. The rooms seemed barely inhabited. Dust and smoke had settled onto the lampshades and windowsills in an ancient way, no longer stirred by the current of wind from the doors.

There was little talk between us that I remember. Nothing seemed safe to offer or ask, as though any question or observation might open a wound, tear the fabric of the present and its fragile balance. I could not say why. There was a tenuousness about the lives lived out in those rooms, some secret kept trapped under the yellowed doilies and mud-stained rugs.

After dinner I helped David's youngest sister wash the dishes. She was a tall girl, maybe fourteen, with long hair and glasses—her resemblance to me at her age was startling. I watched David through the window as he made a tour of the weed-ridden backyard, hands in his pockets, the bones of his elbows and shoulders sharp beneath his flannel shirt. He looked suddenly old, worn-out. He must feel responsible, I thought, the only son, the keeper of the family.

When David came back in, I asked if I could see where his room had been. He led me down a flight of dark stairs, into a small, damp space without windows. Perhaps I'd expected to see the memorabilia of his boy's life—team posters, an old football, deer antlers hung with baseball caps. Instead, there was a sagging bed and little else.

"Do you have any pictures?" I asked. I wanted some insight into his life, some proof that we'd walked the same high school hallways, smoked pilfered Marlboros on the same corner lots. He pulled a trunk from the shallow closet, and I felt a twinge of anticipation. He opened it slowly, and what he pulled out was not a yearbook or the stiff, embroidered letters of an athlete, but a cardboard box that jingled with what I thought must be jewelry. Inside, I found a jumble of insignia and medals. I looked at him.

"Vietnam," he said, as though in that small container, in the name of the country itself, lay the answers to all of my questions.

I remembered the peace patches and love beads I'd worn, the POW bracelet, the soldier whose name I'd kept at my pulse. What little else I knew about Vietnam had come via the evening news I watched when visiting my grandmother and from my relatives' rants against "Hanoi Jane" Fonda. In the church parking lot, I'd seen the bumper stickers: AMERICA—LOVE IT OR LEAVE IT. I came to realize that the government, like my father and the church, did not allow dissent. I'd found that this was yet another thing I could not accept, and I'd cast in my lot with the protestors. When news came of the massacre at Kent State, I'd wept and wished that I had been there to bear witness to such horror or to die at the hands of the oppressor. I had a dramatist's bent for the tragic—a crusader, a youth pastor once said, for all the wrong causes.

In David's trunk I found a sheaf of newspaper clippings

that tore between my fingers. I laid them aside and pulled out a photograph. The men I saw there were my age, a year or two out of high school. They looked like boys, all ears and teeth, dirty and slouched in their jungle fatigues, but there was something used-up about them—the way they shrank in on themselves like old men.

David stood over me. I could smell his smoky breath, the sour permeation of fried meat on his clothes.

"Which one's me?" he asked.

I was already looking at the faces, the eyes, the hands that held the M-16's. Some of the men were standing, others kneeling—even their height offered no clue.

"I don't know," I said.

David pointed, and still I struggled to make the connection. The young man I saw looked fragile in his skin. I ran my finger across the smooth face. I raised my eyes and looked at David: his long hair, his beard and mustache untrimmed and thick. Only the mask of his eyes and nose was visible, the narrow slit of his mouth.

I picked up one of the medals, surprised by its weight in my hand.

"What was this for?"

David rose from the bed, felt in his front jeans pocket for his lighter. "I was a gunner," he said, "on a Huey."

I shook my head, unversed in the language of war.

"Helicopters," David said. "I shot from the door." He walked to a corner of the room, stood there as though contemplating the walls' triangulation. He was different now, turning away from me, not looking.

"We were under fire. This guy had gone down. I told the

pilot to circle back. I jumped out, grabbed him, dragged him up into the chopper." David shrugged. "Made a big deal out of it. Wasn't anything I thought about. I just did it."

I picked up the bundle of newsprint, saw the word HERO in large print.

"Come on," David said. "I want to get home."

I replaced the medals, the ribbons and pins, folded the box back together, closed the trunk lid. I followed David back up the stairs, through the rooms with their quiet light, seeing the photographs on the walls of young men and women I didn't recognize, their faces, necks, and shoulders airbrushed into gauzy pastels, delicate blues and pinks and yellows, sweaters and ties, pearls and lapels—like the high school portraits of my mother and father during that time before the war that wasn't a war, when the world seemed a sure place, when the soldiers came home to gold stars in the windows. I thought then of the words I myself had used in protest—*Baby killers; Remember My Lai.*

Front line, I know now—the death and suffering, the trauma heaped on men too young to have yet made for themselves a life to balance such terror. What so many brought back with them was not a sense of victory or even pride but a desperate need to continue the methods of escape they'd learned while in country: LSD and heroin, barbiturates and hashish, Jack Daniels and Cuervo Gold. Brought back with them, too, the skills necessary to their survival—the wariness and hair-trigger reactions, the ability to remain silent and still—along with the codes that defined their continued existence: take the pain; extract what pleasure exists in the moment; the whole fucking world is your enemy.

I thought I could save David from the wreckage of his

past, somehow give back to him all that his family and country had stolen. That night, when he dropped me at my door, I reached for his arm when he turned to leave, pulled him gently against me, as though I still believed my touch alone were enough to heal. The porch light caught his eyes as he bent stiffly to accept my kiss, then he stepped away, and I knew that there was nothing I could do or say that would keep him there.

When the lights of his pickup had disappeared around the corner, I found my way through the darkness of my living room and into my kitchen. I did not want the stark brilliance of the lamps and fixtures; if I could not have David with me, what I wanted was muted solitude so that I could think, consider, decipher. I'd never met anyone like him; he seemed nearly unknowable. For that reason alone, he drew me. He was a riddle, a conundrum—one I believed I could understand if I applied myself more diligently.

Sitting on my kitchen counter, the window wide open and letting in the night air, I began to wonder what it would take to make him let go his control. If, only moments before, my own desire had been to salve his emotional wounds, what I felt now had less to do with easing his pain than bringing him to a point of sensual distress. I had to know where his weakness lay; I had to know what might tempt him.

SUMMER COMES EARLY to Lewiston, and the fast heat pulled me to the open doors. The bank was boring me with its rigid schedule; the elderly customers irritated me with the pennies they hoarded and asked me to count.

John, perhaps out of regret or a delayed sense of propriety, continued to show up at my door, sorrowful and longing for things to be as they once were. Whatever claims he had on me were yet another thing I yearned to shake. I worried that David might be offended, put off by such baggage. But rather than demand that I save my attention for him alone, David encouraged me to keep seeing John and to date other men, and if at first I thought this odd, I came to see it as a mark of his maturity and self-confidence.

But there was no one else I wanted to be with, no one whose company I wanted to keep more than David's. With him, I could move freely between those parts of myself that had for so long remained disconnected; with David, I felt independent, nearly equal. I could be both masculine and feminine, physical and cerebral. Unlike some men, he was never intimidated by my knowledge or my questions, whether they pertained to Remingtons or Rastafarianism. Like my father, he was at ease with himself, it seemed, believing that there was nothing he could not know and understand, no place in the world he could not walk. It was not that he said so—there was a certain modesty about him—but it was there, that belief he had in his own absolute presence.

For me, David represented a new life, a life still grounded in the steadying clay of my childhood—the forest, the rituals of the hunt, the patriarchal guidance. He gave me a sense of new direction, away from the boredom, the loneliness, the everyday sameness of workdays and weekends. His job as a truck driver spoke of travel, of journey. He brought me trinkets from Seattle: a small grass basket that smelled of sandalwood; a necklace of threaded shells. He came and went, crossed over and back, and I longed to go with him, free and wandering but not lost. The road was his home, he said. He

was a bum, a hobo on wheels, while I stood like an inmate behind the bars of my cage, nine to five, five days a week. The
windows through which I viewed the world were double-
paned, wired and taped, draped and shaded from ceiling to
floor. The doors were heavy with locks. In the basement the
walk-in safe yawned open each morning, revealing walls of
metal boxes, each doubled-keyed, each holding its priceless
contracts and securities.

I wanted out.

A friend, a local life insurance agent, suggested I try and
get on with her company. It sounded wonderful: make my
own hours (sleep in, work late), take prospective clients to
lunch, have my own office and phone, be free of immediate
supervision and the daily pressure of counting every last
dime. All I had to do was convince people they needed a policy. I might make enough money to rent a bigger apartment
and buy the little green Mercury Capri I'd seen parked along
the road with a FOR SALE sign in its window.

When I turned twenty that May, David feigned shock. "I
was dating a teenager," he said, and smiled.

Reaching such a milestone gave me even more reason to
shift gears, steer my life toward something less sedate than
tallying and retallying miscalculated bank statements. And
there were other things I longed to leave behind: fueled by
alcohol, the simmering quarrels between John and his father
had turned vicious. When John packed his bags and left
home, his mother called me. "It's your fault," she said. "You
talked him into this. You've turned him against us."

I gave up protesting. Let them blame me, I thought. It
would make it easier on all of us. Now I had an excuse: John's
mother hated me; we wouldn't be able to work together. I

placed the phone in its cradle, waited a few seconds, then dialed Mr. Paul. I told him I was quitting. I wouldn't be there to open come Monday.

I never said good-bye to Charlene, who might have told me a thing or two about the course my life was taking. Perhaps she had been there already. Perhaps she knew I wouldn't have listened.

I SOLD MY IMPALA and took out a loan on the Capri. I cashed in my benefits from the bank and bought a convincing briefcase, an A-line skirt that meant business, and a pair of solidly built pumps. I left my sink at the window and moved into a larger apartment with a shower, garbage disposal, and air conditioning, part of a complex inhabited mostly by elderly women who tended their sidewalk gardens with meticulous care. Hollyhocks, marigolds, double-blooming mums, parsley, lavender, and chives sprung up around every corner bedroom except mine. I knew they disapproved of everything about me—John's sporadic midnight knocking at my door, his loud imploring, David's shoulder-length hair—and I knew as well that they kept a sharp eye on all my comings and goings. I would see the red gingham curtains of Mrs. Daniels, my closest neighbor, part with a jerk, then drop in decisive disgust. I ignored her scowls as David helped me ferry my belongings, ignored her repeated rap of protest against the wall as David helped me hammer together my bedstead and hang my rifle rack on the wall. I was pleased that he was there to see me reappointing my life, on my way toward something better.

The next week I began making calls to relatives and high

school classmates. I met them for lunch, for drinks after work. I showed up in my new clothes, stylishly dressed. I paid for their sandwiches and beer, sold a few policies. The insurance company fronted me a loan until my commission came through, which I spent to catch up on utilities and car payments. When that was gone, I called my creditors, got extensions, promised full payment soon. I lived on Top Ramen and toast. I smoked away my hunger. On Wednesdays David took me out for dinner, and sometimes he cooked for me, his lean body bent over the oven, pulling out venison roast and pepper gravy.

It was not until the heart of the summer that I realized there was a reason my accounts weren't soaring; I was not comfortable cajoling people into buying what I was selling. It wasn't worth it, I thought—the hours spent going through high school annuals, newspaper announcements of births and marriages, the phone book. The perpetual pleasantries, the superficial conversations, the veneer of goodwill and genuine interest. Even when the contracts were signed, the sheaf of papers folded and tucked into its vinyl cover, I felt less fulfillment than I did phoniness. I left the office nearly nauseous, unable to imagine the next call, the next meeting, the next sincerity-laced pitch, until, finally, I sat for hours in front of the telephone, thinking that I'd dial the number in five more minutes, then ten, waiting for the courage and conviction that never came.

Instead, I called my cousin Les and asked her to meet me for a drink. I'd already hit Les up for a $10,000 policy. She'd taken out $20,000 instead, betting she'd die before the company could realize a dime off her premiums. A year out of high school, she was living with Marc, once a state-champion wrestler and now a lumberjack, a man I believed might hold his own against her if push came to shove.

We met at the Airport Lounge, where we sat drinking Fogcutters—thick, green concoctions made of seven different kinds of alcohol that went down easy. Drink four, the bar's mantra went, and if you can still walk, the fifth one's on us. There were bills to pay, yet here I was, spending my last ten dollars on a surefire hangover.

I told Les I couldn't stand the calls to friends, asking for a few minutes of their time, peddling policies for something no one really wanted to think about. *Let's talk about death, or perhaps only dismemberment, the loss of a limb or an eye.* I felt like a parasite, sucking away whatever goodwill existed between me and those I could only see as potential clients.

"To hell with selling insurance," Les said. "Do something else."

"Like what? What else is there to do in this town?"

"I don't know," Les said. "Be a secretary or something."

What I knew about Les was that she would never sell life insurance or be a secretary. Les's goals ran toward risk and wealth, and the men in that room knew it; the swish of her legs crossing stopped their conversations mid-sentence. I envied the ease of her command, the way she both absorbed and ignored the men's concentrated attention.

We drank ourselves into bravery that night, the kind of bravery we needed to go home and face the lives we had fashioned for ourselves. Sometimes, when Marc and David were working out of town, Les and I spent the night together as we had when we were girls, sleeping in the same bed, whispering our secrets long past midnight. But the secrets we told were no secrets at all—the true secrets would come later, in the years ahead when Les's life would twist and contort into a knotted story only she can tell, and my own life would become a narrative of shame.

THE NEXT WEEK I dressed in my newest pantsuit—pink polyester with satin trim—tucked my briefcase under my arm, and drove to David's apartment. He would make me dinner while I sold him on the benefits of a policy with Northwestern Mutual.

I'd drawn up a contract for $70,000 of whole-life, pleased with myself for daring such a high figure, probably more than he needed, but he could afford it. My commission would be enough to keep the creditors at bay for another month, give me room to rethink my direction.

I watched David negotiate the small kitchen, watched the way he leaned himself against the counter, the smooth movement of his fingers as he separated the lettuce, peeled the spuds to milky whiteness. I liked the feeling of being waited on by a man who didn't seem to mind time over the stove. Deer meat from the previous fall, potatoes fried with onions, canned corn or peas on the side, a bottle of wine, Riunite or Lancer's—nothing beyond what I was accustomed to. I savored the thinly cut venison, savored not only the mild wildness but the taste memory that brought with it the familiarity of past family dinners.

When I looked at David sitting next to me, this is what I saw: a man who knew what I knew, whose senses responded to the same smells and sounds, the same tastes I had known all my life. He seemed to embody everything I had treasured and lost, yet there was more to him than anything I had left behind: he was both recognizable and strange, comfort and compulsion. He was the projection of myself, a masculine reflection of my own codes and inspirations.

The distance that remained between us puzzled me. David still hadn't touched me that I can remember, and I think that I would. But if I can't remember what came before that evening, I will never forget what came after.

We were sitting on his couch, watching an HBO special. I was a little light-headed from my glass of wine, yet very aware of his presence beside me, he at one end of the sofa, I at the other. Each time he reached to adjust the volume or pour more wine, I felt my breath catch, the heat that came between us.

Las Vegas was on the screen, showgirls with their feathers and bare breasts. I watched with embarrassment, both at the display and at my being bashful about it. (HBO was the underground in Lewiston, Idaho, 1978; in another few years MTV would blow us away.) It was the first time I'd seen nudity onscreen. Once again I felt David watching me, gauging my reaction.

It would be a lie to say I wasn't aroused, less by the show than by his eyes on me. The eyes not of a lecher but of a discerner, a practiced and particular intelligence. What excited me had to do with unspeakable possibility. Whatever rules had governed me fell away in his presence because this was his game, and my first time at his table. I was waiting, for what I wasn't sure. But now I could feel it about to happen, each minute drawing me nearer to the knowing.

David began to speak to me then, in a way that was more direct, more intense than he had before. Had I ever looked at pornography? he asked. Yes, I answered, but I did not tell him of the books Les and I had found in our uncle's room. What I mentioned instead were John's occasional *Playboy*, a single, tattered *Playgirl* a friend had gotten at her wedding shower. He smiled. No, not that kind. He went into his bedroom and came back with magazines, women splayed and rouged, tipped up for the camera, tipped back for the men who held their knees.

A page, a level at a time, he took me down, until what I saw before me bore no resemblance to the airbrushed depictions of Ivy League girls gone bad for the weekend. What I remember are the colors—smoky black, lacquered red.

As I thumbed through the magazines, David told me of the topless dancers and prostitutes in Seattle he had met and befriended during the twelve-hour layovers of his truck route. He made me understand that they waited for his arrival, that what he gave to them overshadowed anything they might offer. I was intrigued. Why would this man court me as he had, so modestly, if he were the Don Juan of Puget Sound? Why would he want *me*?

He pulled me from the couch and led me to his bedroom. I felt his hands for the first time, gentle, he said, because this was the beginning and there would be more, but gentle for now so that I would learn how much I must trust him.

THIS IS WHAT I KNOW of seduction: it can be flowered and perfumed, or it can spring from sweat and darkness; it can come sweet and slow, or fast and hard like birth. It can find you at work or at home, awake or asleep. It can begin with a kiss or the withholding of a kiss. It's a flower that opens, a bruise that spreads.

For each of us, there exists the possibility of being seduced, and for each of us, two kinds of seduction. The first is
romantic and hoped for; the second is perhaps the truer, its
shape less familiar, its tenets less defined. When in it, we
don't know where we're headed, what to protest, how to protect ourselves. It's like being led blind down a dark corridor,
yet when you stop to push against the walls, they disappear,
and you are free. Can't you see? Free.

 THE MYSTERIOUSNESS, THE HIDDEN store of knowledge—I believed that physical intimacy was David's way of allowing me entrance into his life. Although he still said little about his family and his past, he began to speak openly about his former lovers, and I saw that sharing his bed allowed me to share his confidence. As I listened to his detailed stories of marathon lovemaking, jealous husbands, risky rendezvous, I sensed that he was gauging my response, watching me for signs of jealousy or possessiveness. I sensed, too, that such response would not please him.

We talked frankly of sexual experience and technique, and for the first time I was able to express myself openly, candidly. David was not covetous of my past, nor did he respond with juvenile lechery. He listened as calmly and pleasantly as though I were reciting my school lessons, nodding his encouragement. Perhaps we spoke of the ridiculous nature of monogamy, the artificial construct of marriage. Perhaps we agreed on the merits of sexual freedom, some intellectualized form of the *free love* I had romanticized as a teenager, when I'd longed to be with the hippies in Haight-Ashbury. David was an anarchist, and in my zealous bid for my own social and spiritual emancipation, he seemed a wise and worthy guide, the engine that would carry me toward my destination.

One night he opened the top drawer of his bureau; it was a treasure chest of sex toys, condoms, foams and jellies—a grown-up version of the pediatrician's trunk of goodies that I was allowed to rummage through after braving my weekly allergy shot.

"What's your preference?" he asked, but I was too amazed and too shy to risk a response. He laughed, patted the bed beside him. "You don't have to do anything you don't want to do. We don't even have to have sex. We can just lie here and talk. It's up to you."

I felt enormous relief and gratitude. David's generosity convinced me that I was on a new and wonderful path. Here was a man with whom I could explore the sexual forest without fear of judgment or reprisal. There were a few times at first when I tested the truth of his words: what would he do if I said no? How many times would he lie beside me with only a light touch of hands between us? But he held steady. His mood, his contentment, seemed to have little to do with me, though I could tell he took pleasure in my company. Perhaps it was his age, his maturity and experience, that accounted for the absence of slavering eagerness. He never mewled or humped or pouted. I felt as though I had been liberated, as though, finally, I was with a man who would not depend upon me to pacify. Liberated, too, from that sense of myself as possession, for David made it clear that he would not ask me to belong only to him.

But who else would I choose to be with? No one held my interest like David; no one offered the kind of possibility that he did. Yet I didn't consider "falling in love" with David. Ours was a practical and unencumbered union, and I liked it that way. Although much of our intimate time together revolved around discussion and demonstration of sexual variation, I found that what excited me about David had little to do with the physical. My arousal was intellectual. It was the *knowing* that lured me, that deep current that pulled me farther away from shore. Secrets, things hidden and unspoken, the moon's shadowed face: I believed that there was nothing that I did not want to observe and understand, no knowledge that I did not yearn to possess. My body was the decoy, my mind the open maw. *Feed me*, I said to David, and he did.

WHAT I FELT in the beginning, then, was strength, sureness, new power, exalted independence. We hunted and fished, cooked together, read together, entertained each other long into the night and never spoke of the next day or month or year except in terms of activity and destination. If we did not love each other, we loved what we shared together, and I began to wonder if this wasn't the more blessed state. When my karate lessons conflicted with his nights home, I quit the class, unwilling to miss out on a chance to share David's company.

Our time in public had about it an air of jubilation. David was a movable feast of hedonistic indulgence. People were *joyful* around him. His was perhaps the truest laugh I have ever heard, and when I picture him, even now, he is that man I first came to know, giddy as a child when something pleases him, his smile so full it wrinkles his eyes and sets him to bouncing with glee.

Our out-on-the-town fun was freewheeling if dangerous: barreling from one bar to the next, meeting friends and drinking tequila slammers—a shot glass of Cuervo and soda banged down on the table, creating a head of foam that we drank in one swallow. It was the incense of marijuana, which I seldom smoked but all those around me clamored for: I loved to be with them in the basements, bathrooms, and backseats as they broke into gales of raucous laughter. It was the dancing, dancing, dancing at our town's first disco. The lights were everywhere: the floor itself pulsing, the strobes, the mirrored ball hung from the ceiling reflecting it all back in a shower of color. Sometimes we huddled inside the glass sound booth, where the deejay shared with us his tiny vials of amyl nitrate. We closed the place down six nights a week, swaying in line through the Hustle with John Travolta wannabes (bull-necked farm boys jabbing the air), drunk on Pink Cadillacs and Wet Dreams and whatever other mixture of alcohol and syrup the bartender could concoct.

Or we went to Modern West, a cowboy bar with a slick floor large enough to accommodate a small village of couples engaged in controlled collisions. I mingled in my shiny dress and strappy high heels, smug among the pearl-buttoned cow-girls twirling in their Lady Wranglers. I learned to brace my-self against the pull and thrust of Western swing, sore the next morning from being snapped and retrieved by ropey-armed cowboys.

When last call came, we stepped out into the street, be-numbed by alcohol and the absence of light, possessed of a sudden and deep unwillingness to do anything but continue what the evening had begun. The word would go out that there was a party, and for a time the party was always at

David's. He had rented a new and expensive apartment closer to downtown, in an upscale complex, pool and hot tub included.

The crowd was made up of men and women I knew or knew of, whose faces were familiar because I had seen them around town: grocery clerks and lawyers, sales reps and waitresses, some pushing middle age, others too young to be legal. The gatherings had an underground feel to them, as though what brought people to the door—and got them through it—were a secret code, some cryptic tattoo. Uneasy with the pounding music, the cocaine lined out on the bathroom vanity, I'd watch and sip at my gin.

"You're too tight," David would tell me, rubbing my back. He didn't like to see me turn down a good high, he said. "Loosen up, have fun. I'll take care of you." I'd smile, assuring him that I wasn't the drudge, the straightlaced church girl I'd once been.

David introduced me to his male friends with obvious satisfaction, but instead of remaining close by, demonstrating his attachment, he would smile encouragingly, then turn his attention to another cluster of people. I wasn't used to such autonomy. Tom and John had hovered at my side like guard dogs, fierce and territorial, sniffing the air for rival scent. David's benign behavior reminded me more of Thane, who had governed me with equanimity and had never been threatened by other men. In fact, David seemed to view me much as Thane had: not as a *girlfriend,* a love interest, but as an affectionate compatriot. I was a good traveling companion, game for adventure, not given to petty grievances and suffocating restrictions. I had succeeded in remaking myself into that hybrid I believed might grant me the greatest access into the world of men: a masculine spirit and intellect; a feminine body and libido. With my mind, I challenged and prevailed; with my sex, I appeased and confirmed. It was a delicate balance, easily upset should I fail to abide by the rules, and one of those rules was that I would not be like other women; I would demand nothing that might impinge upon the man's license to live his life free of female imposition.

So that when, one evening, I missed David's presence at the party and found him standing in the kitchen, sheltered by the refrigerator's open door, his back to its interior, I did not hesitate when he motioned me forward. There, I watched a girl I'd gone to school with kneel before him, her face damp and eerily blue in the cold light. I did not turn away because I couldn't: I was mesmerized by what I was seeing, and I knew as well that my presence was linked to David's pleasure. I also knew that it was not simply the young woman who had tantalized David: it was the proximity of those who might find them, the possibility, the hope of being discovered. My role was to bear witness, even as David kept his eyes on me, for I was the one on whom the perfection of the moment depended.

I watched until I heard a distant voice ask where I was, and when I left the kitchen and entered the larger room of people, I felt dizzy and breathless, as though I'd just stepped off a carnival ride. I knew they were still in there, and that others might find them, and I was both alarmed and exalted by the possibility. When after a time the young woman came from the kitchen, and then David behind her, I lowered my eyes, perhaps out of some residual shame, although the emotions that filled me were too numerous and disparate to name. I sparked with the charge of negative and positive, the push and pull of learned rejection and curious accommodation. When David made his way to my side, he smiled down at me and nodded as though confirming the delicious secret between us, and I felt my identity shift. I was no longer an artless young woman, a Lewiston girl, a tentative purveyor of light pleasure. I was a coconspirator, a partner in the confederacy of the senses.

Later that night, David urged me to tell him exactly what I had seen, what I had felt. He filled in his own details—her tongue, her teeth, the nape of her neck. Together, we spoke the story again and again, gave it color and texture, until I believed that I had not simply watched but had been there with them, in that harbor of blue light and cool air.

When, at the next party, I watched David ascend the stairs to his bedroom, another woman at his side, I didn't lower my eyes but poured myself another shot of schnapps and lit another cigarette, biding my time. There were those who looked at me with pity, but I met their gaze with studied nonchalance. I knew that, when the evening was over, I would be the one left in David's bed, and that I would possess the secrets of the women who had long since staggered to their cars alone.

I believed that this was a private and privileged thing between David and me. Any confusion I felt was replaced with David's assurance that this, indeed, was what he wanted: my observation, my passive participation. When David touched me, I believed that I became for him the embodiment of every mouth and breast, the manifestation, the fulfillment of his truest need.

But what was it that I wanted from David? The answer

came to me clearly: not devotion, not domestic provision, but companionship. I wanted to be in his presence; I wanted the gift of his attention, the gratification of being his confidante, the one on whom he could depend. I wanted to be different from the other women he had told me about who had failed him, fickle and easily wounded; I wanted to be the antithesis of the female defined for me by the church, by my own family, by the books whose priggish heroines teased and withheld.

This was what kept me there—not the sex, not even the perception that I was winning David with my tolerance and patience—but the belief that I was setting myself apart, escaping my fate, ascending to a higher level of insight. Anything less would disappoint this man who had chosen me to accompany him toward discovery, who depended upon me to share the transcendence of his vision.

With David, there was no denial, no boundaries, or so it seemed. Over the next several months, those boundaries would become more clear. They were *his* boundaries, and though they bore no resemblance to the rules I had been raised to abide by, they were no less absolute.

Perhaps I believed that I could exist at the margins, that I could walk away whenever I chose, just as I had walked away from the house of my father, that I could pack my bags and step through that door, shrug off my fetters, and begin a new journey.

I wonder now when my sense of that journey changed. I wonder when it was I first heard the shades being drawn against the light, the doors closing, the slow, metallic clicking of locks.

———

EARLY SUMMER. I lay one evening in the sleeper of David's semi, listening to his easy banter with the shift workers. It was the first time David had offered to take me with him to Seattle, and we were docked to pick up our load and head west.

The tractor was a twenty-one-gear Freightliner, pulling a single trailer from Lewiston to Pasco, double from there into Tacoma/Seattle. My presence in the sleeper was a secret because no riders were allowed, and I spent the first few miles hidden behind the coarse black curtain that divided the cab. A pillow, a blanket thrown over a thin pad—nothing like other sleepers I'd seen at the car shows, with their king-size beds, walls plushly lined with fake fur and velveteen drapes. My Spartan quarters smelled of old smoke, unlaundered linen, moisture sweated and pooled against vinyl.

Between Washington's eastern border and the ocean lie miles of scrubland, desert dry, blown with sage. The mountains that surround the river drainages—the Blues, the Cascades—seemed impossibly distant. We pulled the trip between dusk and dawn, and my sense of that land has less to do with terrain and sky than it does with the few feet of highway our headlights illuminated.

The moon rose like white heat, the rock fired in silver. Coyotes became foolish then, separating themselves from shadow, feeding on the small animals flushed out of hiding by the false sun. I could look across the cab and see David's face, see his one hand on the wheel, cigarette in the other. I felt giddy, as though I had been given flight.

I discovered the night world of long-haul truckers wired on coffee, NoDoz, amphetamines—whatever it took to pull through hundreds of miles of darkness. Some spent their hours on the CB, radioing other truckers ahead or behind, calling up the locals whose towns they passed through. Others tuned in to preachers broadcasting their message of salvation, praying along as the mile markers flew by and the sun coming up seemed another kept promise.

That first night, when we pulled into one of the twenty-four-hour cafés that anchored the freeway, I lowered my eyes beneath the appraising looks of men at the counter. I found their gaze sinister and embarrassing, but David saw in their stares a validation of his judgment.

It is hard to remember myself there, in the white-yellow light of glass and fluorescence; not *hard* but painful, because what I see is a girl dressed in a dancer's leotard, tight jeans, and high heels, balanced on a bar stool between men who hunch around her. They've got their elbows alongside their plates, their boots planted on the linoleum. Their hands are rough, their faces lined from the efforts of smoking and squinting through hours of fog, sunlight, hail. As David nudges me in front of him, tells me to straighten my back and lick my lips, I'm thinking that this is all a game, that David will protect me because it is he who has made up the rules.

"They're wishing they had what I have," he said later, patting my bottom as we walked from the brightly lit diner, and because some part of me responded to both his desire and his insistence on theirs, I let myself believe that I might please him this way. I did not let myself think of those other drivers as men like my father, men with wives and daughters and sons, men who whispered not of my desirability but of my misfortune. Perhaps they even worried over me, seeing I was young and obviously ignorant. Many of them knew David, had seen him over the years in the same cafés, the same truck stops and rest areas, had seen his way with women and the kind of women he chose to share his bed.

Back in the truck, he told me I'd done fine. Next time I should wear something more revealing, something that would show them my tits. He lit a cigarette, smiled and winked.

There was nothing outside my window then but the charcoal silhouette of black trees against black sky. We were speeding toward Seattle, toward the ocean, toward people I'd never seen, land I'd never touched, water I'd never tasted. I meant to do that, taste the bay's water and see if the salt were a true thing.

I cracked the window an inch. The wind came in full of forest smells as we climbed Snoqualmie Pass, and I had a sudden, nauseating ache for my family, for my child's life spent cloistered in the woods, but that life was no longer mine.

Then who was I? The logger's daughter come down from the mountains who hated her own ignorance of the world. A skinny, stubborn, strong-willed girl who needed to be broken, needed to learn. I didn't know which side my bread was buttered on, didn't know that if I wanted to dance, I'd have to pay the fiddler.

And that was the name—the truck driver's handle—that David gave me so that I might be known on the waves of the air. "Tiny Dancer," he whispered when I pleased him. "Dance."

In the months to come, I would learn the complex shifting of gears, throwing my weight to the clutch, feeling the engine shudder and grind beneath me. I would learn the parlance of shortwave, the rhythms and code of numbers and names. Sometimes, listening to the voices floating in from the trucks and houses miles away, I felt as though I were a foreigner, the language not my own. The land was unfamiliar, my sense of time reversed, nocturnal. My family had no idea where I was, and I could not have said I knew the man who sat beside me. I would soon forget that I had ever been anyone else, that I had kissed with passion born of love, that I had once been touched by a lover whose hands held comfort.

Seattle, to me, will always be that city I first came to know not by its proximity to water nor its rain, but by First Street, the lineup of sex stores where David took me soon after our arrival. Seattle is a cramped booth with a machine that takes quarters for five minutes of flesh, filmed or sometimes live. Seattle is row after row of sex toys and magazines glistening with skin that has been pierced, tattooed, injected, impaled. Seattle is a cheap motel where truckers pay by the hour for a bed and curtains to draw against the light. It is a topless bar where women cup their breasts and lower themselves onto the laps of customers, women who, when they saw him, welcomed David not as a john but as a lover, as someone whose attention meant more to them than money.

This was the life he offered me, and even as he whispered with the women and I saw them take me in, something between jealousy and amusement in their eyes, I never thought to run.

From that first trip to Seattle on, during the nighttime hauls, during the days meant for sleep but fueled into wakefulness by speed, during all those times when his desire for me became a ritual of domination, I would do what David asked; I would become for him the woman I believed I must be.

"WHAT DO YOU WANT ME TO DO?"

"It's not what I want you to do. It's what *you* want to do."

We lay on David's bed, in the breeze coming in from the patio door, open to the cool air of midnight. I took the joint that he offered, pinched it between my fingers. I pretended to take the smoke into my lungs, pretended to hold my breath. In the dark, he couldn't see that the motions were false, that the smoke drifted free of my mouth. I didn't want escape, disorientation. I wanted this moment with David, just the two of us, the wind smelling of the river, the muddy shallows. I wanted us to talk of other things—I wanted to hear the stories of his youth, of Vietnam. I wanted to know how his father had left and why. I wanted him to tell me what lay deepest in his mind, what wonders held him just before sleep, what answers came before waking.

I listened as David's voice softened. I liked him high because it was the only time he seemed able to rest, the only time the rigidity left him, and I could reach out and touch him with tenderness. There had been so little lingering of lips at the throat's pulse, so few caresses; I do not remember his kiss at all. Each movement had its purpose, as if part of a well-rehearsed play, intentional and detached. He shied away from my eyes held too long on his; he turned his back when what I wanted was only to hold him.

This was not what David wanted—not the arm-linking, not the lush kiss or the spooning sleep of lovers. What he wanted, he said—more, even, than my voyeur's eye and ear—was to have me lie with other men, men he would designate and direct. Our conversations had come down to this one thing: when would I be ready?

"I don't know," I said. "I don't think I can bring myself to do that."

"Quit thinking about it," he said. "Just do it. The first time is the hardest. After that it's easy."

There was the encouragement of his smile, the sureness in his words that meant he believed I would do the right thing—and that right thing would be to step out of my old skin and into the new, free myself from the old parables of temptation and punishment. I needed to test my wings, he said. I needed to fly.

I felt a certain curiosity, but I cannot say I felt a true sexual urge toward such an encounter. My interest lay not in other men but in David. Yet how could I separate the two? Everything I knew about men and women revolved around this one truth: to keep a man happy, a woman must meld her will to his, become for him the extension and fulfillment of his need.

"Is that what you really want?" I spoke into the darkness of the room, smelling the sweet smoke, feeling as though I'd been unleashed from my mooring, floating toward deeper waters.

He tucked me against him, ran the length of his palm across my face. He held me for a long time, nothing more.

And then, after a time, he rose, pulled me gently after him. Already there was someone waiting in the next room, someone who had been there all along. I had not known this. I had believed us alone, believed myself free to contemplate and consider without consequence. I'd forgotten how well he knew this road, how he was always there ahead of me, preparing the way that I should go.

"COME HERE," he would say, and I would. Then he would tell me what he wanted. Sometimes he wanted me to do nothing more than undress for him. On the dance floor, he instructed me to move my hips, arch my back, tilt my shoulders. He scolded me for sunbathing in my swimsuit: the unattractive tan lines marred my skin. Sometimes, when another man asked me to dance, I would look up and see David where he sat at our table, encircled by friends, watching me, smiling, nodding his approval, pleased with his creation.

A kind of Bacchus, reduced to bone, running on whiskey and speed, he brought us together cheerfully, as though what we were about was a communal celebration. The ones left at the night's end were the most or least hardened, the reduction of time and sobriety. These were the men I would come to fear most: those who knew what they were capable of, and those who, as of yet, did not.

It is this story that I sometimes believe I cannot speak, the darkest moments of my passage. Even now I cloak the truth of it in vagaries. What is it I mean to tell? How can I define what it is that I longed for, what emotion directed me?

If I tear through the curtain of words, I see *love,* so easily, rend first, then *need, curiosity, desire, lust.* The story is about all these things and none of them—it is about what these words become when they are no longer words but currency on the tongue.

It is not simply the sex that shamed me. I understand how the wondrous exploration of sensual delight can be twisted into something disgraceful, so that even a chaste woman in her marriage bed will cringe in mortification at her body's sanctified quickening. All the warnings, the broadcast of admonitions concerning carnal pleasure, the insistence on separation of body and soul, the inherent weakness of the clay vessel forever compromising the ethereal spirit—even now I struggle to free myself of the spectral jury, sitting in judgment of my pleasure.

But this is not about sex. It is about confusion bred into fear; it is about the tyranny built on that fear—controlling the body, the mind, the soul of another. It is about being raised to believe that women want to be, must be, dominated. It is about rejecting those beliefs and still being unable to escape them—so wide a river, so many currents to swim through.

I thought I was near the surface when I met David Jenkins. No more father, no more church, no more concerns about what others might think. David was my guide into the new world; by the time I realized I was lost, the last swell of land had fallen away from beneath my feet.

What I mean to say is this: there are rooms in which a girl

with hair the color of caramel licks the thighs of her lover's lover. Rooms full of people who will bind one another and bite small moons into flesh, and they will do this not out of love or lust but out of a need to reduce by half the pain they themselves are feeling, and to override by half the pain the other is feeling, and it will never be enough. There is a room with a bed on which two people will make a simple love and the one will go home and gag and purge himself with emetics and thrash himself and spend in the lovely rage of his guilt.

And that other: she may sleep and dream; she may wake up charmed. She may crawl thirst-stricken from that bed to the bed of another, believing, even then, that she will not survive the desert of her journey.

THERE WERE THOSE WHO WOULD TRY to save me. John came for me once, walked through the door of David's apartment, took the stairs two at a time, ignoring the revelers and their beery questions. I was in David's bed, drunk and sick on tequila, perhaps sedated by the Quaaludes he'd threatened to slip into my drinks. I'd curled myself tight beneath the sheets, the loud music and laughter reaching me in waves as I drifted in and out of sleep.

I recognized John's touch, the clean smell of him. He was stroking my hair, calling my name. "I'm getting you out of here," he said, and he pulled the sheet from the bed, wrapping it around me and lifting me to his chest. I felt like I was floating, tethered to his arms by thin bits of cloth as we descended the stairs into the heat and noise, the sweet smoke, the charged air.

The laughter quieted; only the music, the drum and shrill guitar, John's voice, then David's. I remember wondering if David would let me go, if he would let John take me. Everyone in that room was afraid of John, his size and the fierceness with which he stared them down, dared them to stand in his way. But something in me welled up then, some impulse to fight my own fight, hold my own ground. I tried to say it strongly, but it came out as a whisper: "Take me back upstairs, John. Please don't do this to me."

What is it like to hold a woman in your arms, the whole of her, to move with her easily from one place to the next, while the room of people watches to see you relinquish your possession? Because John did, he did what I begged him to do. He turned and moved back up the stairs slowly, and David followed, waiting as John laid me gently down and covered me again.

What words then passed between them I don't remember. Sleep was there, and I let its current take me, away from the final sadness on John's face, away from his lips on mine.

THERE IS ANOTHER BOY, whose lover I was for an hour, no more. He is the one whose face I will remember, whose eyes will bring me back into myself for a single, excruciating moment, while the party roars on and David waits patiently in the next room. He is the one who has been chosen and sent to me, whom I must receive. He comes to where I sit on the cedar bench of the sauna, hesitates when the door behind him closes. He kneels before me, then rests his head in the cleft of my hands, the fingered lap I have made for him.

Long, blond hair falls across his bare shoulders. His eyes

are a delicate blue. He is fair, fine-boned, so fragile as I hold him and wait. He trembles and I lift his chin. I see how it is with him. He is crying. He thinks he must love me.

He is afraid for me. Or of me. How can I soothe him? He is older than I, perhaps twenty-three. I touch his forehead, let my hands slide beneath his arms, pull him toward me. He comes to me easily, he is a child, and I take him and hold him and rock him there, the two of us alone in the mist of the rocks that shush and whisper.

This will be our secret, this moment of nothing. It is our secret and David must not know, for this is an intimacy he cannot give or receive and is a betrayal I must not risk. This is injury, infidelity, treason. Yet, in this other one's eyes, I have seen myself, the pity and fear, the tender regard, the power I possess and contain.

I hold to him until the heat is too little or too much, until we must rise together and go from that room and say to the man who waits, "We are done."

10 A WARM AFTERNOON IN SEATTLE, JUST outside Pike Place Market, where David and I had gone for a lunch of smoked salmon. We might have been any other couple walking the wharf that day, smiling in the coastal sun, feeding the seagulls our scraps. This was the part of Seattle I loved, the city I'd romanticized as a girl while watching *Here Come the Brides* on my grandmother's TV, singing along with the theme song: "The bluest skies you've ever seen in Seattle. . . ." I hummed the words as David and I stopped at the import shops, where I bought bamboo baskets and sandalwood incense, willing myself to forget that we had just come from First Avenue and its sex shops, whose wares David preferred over the cheap knickknacks I adored.

On our way back to the parking lot, in an open, concrete stairway, we came upon a large man beating a hooker; the bitch, he shouted to the gawking crowd, owed him money.

We stood and watched with everyone else as the pimp raised his fists again and again, as the girl slumped against the metal banister, slid down the concrete wall, blood on her face, blood in her hands. I started toward them, thinking I could stop the man from hitting, thinking I could somehow save her.

"Don't," David said, and grabbed my arm.

"Why doesn't someone do something?" I pulled away, saw the pimp wipe his fist in the handkerchief he'd taken from his pocket. People turned their heads, witness to nothing.

"That's none of our business," David said. He began walking. I looked at the woman, who lay crying on the landing between stairs. People stepped carefully around her.

"The main thing you've got to remember," David said as we drove back toward the motel, "is that she was a whore. She wasn't worth it."

I stared out the window as we passed the King Dome, the Space Needle, the museum with its long lines—thousands waiting to see the sarcophagus of King Tut. It was late, and we needed to pick up our load and head toward home. I was sick with what I had witnessed—both the violence and David's unwillingness to intervene. I was beginning to understand how carefully David weighed his risks—a skill he'd honed in the jungles of Vietnam. He had survived, come back alive after two tours of duty, the first one because he'd been drafted and forced to go, the second because he had lived through the first and was now good at this game of war. What home offered him was minimum wage and laws he would rather not keep. In 'Nam he had all the drugs he could eat, and the women there did not know the word for love.

"TELL ME WHAT IT WAS LIKE," I asked David. "Tell me about Vietnam." I lay in the dark with my head on his shoulder, listening as he spoke of the long bunkered nights of shelling, how the men lined up cigarette butts, one after another balanced on end, knowing that when they tipped from

the mortars' concussion it was time to *bug out*. He spoke of
the men and the huts they called hooches, of the young, local
girls they shared, who did their laundry, swept the dirt clean
of straw and leaves, gave the soldiers whatever sex they
wanted for a few bucks a month. He remembered their small
mouths, their smooth, hairless bodies.

"Was there one who was special?" I asked.

"That wouldn't work," David said. "Some would fuck you,
then mine the dumps."

"Then what?"

David let out a slow breath, the smoke rising from his
mouth, a dry mist in the light from the street. I waited for his
answer but heard only the beat of his heart slowing toward
sleep.

THE MORE TIME I SPENT with David, the less anything
else seemed to matter. What women friends I had left were
not friends but partners, caught up in the orbit of David's
pull. We convened at the bars to drink, we gathered in the
bathrooms to scrape together our miniature windrows of cocaine, line our numbing lips with ochre and mahogany,
brush our cheekbones to a deeper shade of rose. We were in
the business of feeling good, looking good, making of the
night something sharp, something brilliant, before the music
ended.

Even those occasional afternoons I spent with my grandmother, sheltered by her venetian blinds and ruffled curtains, the walls collaged with family photographs, were not
enough to pull me back from the edge. Nan would lie on her
couch, surrounded by the details of her life: iced tea, tissue,

lotion, nail file, past issues of *Reader's Digest,* a fluted bowl of hard candies. Always at hand was the small box with its cards of various colors, each citing a biblical verse. As I child, I had loved the morning ritual of closing my eyes, running my fingers across the cards' stacked ridge, choosing the one piece of Scripture that would guide my day.

Those few hours spent with my grandmother were made fragile by the absence of what had once held between us— the easy habits of cleaning, the endless games of checkers, during which she would fall asleep until I jostled her into her next move. Now we watched television, which demanded nothing of us except attention to its blue-lit box. *Dialing for Dollars, The Price Is Right, Let's Make a Deal, Jeopardy!:* we encouraged the hesitant, shouted answers at the dumb, berated those who would not take the chance. When I moved to leave, she would beckon me for a kiss, and I would smell the lavender powder, the cologne she touched to her throat each morning, regardless of who might come by. I'd step out into the dull sound of the city, my pockets full of licorice drops and strawberry taffy, and feel like a traitor, a voyeur, a spy, inhabiting one world and stealing from another.

It did not matter which way I drove when I left my grandmother, what structure of wood I chose to call my own. I had built for myself a house without windows. I wanted no one to look in, and I no longer remembered what reason I might have for looking out.

"REMEMBER TO LOCK YOUR DOORS," my mother said. "Keep your curtains closed."

"I will."

"There's a lot of meanness in the world."

I listened, only half hearing the direness of her warnings—I had heard them so many times before.

When I had told her about David, I'd said only that he was a truck driver, that he made good money. When I told her his age, she had made a small noise in the back of her throat. "He's nearly as old as I am, Kim."

I did not tell her that his age was the least of it. There was, in fact, little that I *could* tell her, and into my silence she must have read shame. Every word I uttered seemed a lie.

Still, I sensed some relief on her part: at least I was with one man, not the one she would have chosen for me, but someone I might eventually marry and leave my life of sin, someone who could shelter me from the evil lurking outside—a man to protect me from other men.

I said good-bye and hung up the phone. The sudden stillness sucked my breath away. David was in Seattle, and though he seldom called, I hoped that he might think of me, dial my number from the bar or motel. Sometimes he phoned from the strip joints, and I would hear the music and shouts, the voice of a woman urging him away.

I moved to the couch, covered myself with the colorful afghan my mother had knitted, its squares of blue and brown domestic and contained. The television's picture skittered and jumped, and I closed my eyes, grateful for the voices filling the room.

It was well after ten when I heard the knock at my door. I thought for a moment it might be my neighbor, Mrs. Daniels, who came sometimes to remind me that the next day was garbage pickup or that I had left my laundry in the communal dryer, but she'd surely be sleeping.

When I cracked the door and peered outside, I saw a man in his thirties, dressed in jeans, sweatshirt, and ball cap.

"Hi," he said. "I'm trying to find the apartment of a buddy. We've got a softball game tonight. Could I use your phone to call?"

I hesitated, then shrugged. He looked familiar. Maybe an old friend of John's. "Sure," I said, and pointed toward the kitchen.

He acted a little shy, shuffling and ducking past me. "Do you have a phone book I could use?" he asked.

I watched as he thumbed his way through the pages. He seemed nervous, distracted. Something wasn't right in the way he was searching, as though he had forgotten his reason for doing so.

"What's your friend's name?" I asked. "Maybe I can tell you which apartment he's in."

He hesitated. "Bill Talkington," he said, then quickly flipped the pages to the T's. He found a number and dialed. I can't remember what he spoke into the receiver, but when the call was over, he asked to use my bathroom.

I waited for the toilet to flush. It didn't. I moved quietly into the hall and saw him in my bedroom. He was surveying the walls, the window, the closet, and I thought then he must be a burglar. The only things of value I owned were in that room: my Ithaca shotgun, my Remington 6-mm, my father's 30.06.

A trill of fear caught in my chest. I stepped into the kitchen and coughed. A few seconds later I heard the toilet flush.

He came out with his hands in his pockets, hesitated,

looked around the room as though he had forgotten something. I opened the door, encouraging him outside.

"Thanks," he said, and I smiled with relief, but just as he
stepped onto the porch, he caught the door in his hand,
wedged his foot across the threshold.

"Tell me your name. Just your name."

Fear welled up in me, and I fought to control the waver in
my voice. "Go, or I'll call the police."

The hand withdrew, and then the thick-soled tennis shoe.
I locked the door quickly, then dragged a chair from the
kitchen and wedged it beneath the knob.

I slumped onto the couch. The rush of adrenaline seeped
away, and I suddenly felt overwhelmed by exhaustion. I
wished desperately that David were with me.

What I believed was that David would protect me, and my
belief seems strange to me now. It was David, after all, whose
sexual appetite was fed by the desire I kindled in other men.
It was David whose greed manifested itself in scenes of physical domination. But I knew, too, that it was David who controlled and directed, who chose the beginning and brought
about the end. Above all else, I was his to take or offer; he
would never allow this man his trespass.

I pulled the afghan around my legs and focused on the
television. The screen's blue flickering and the low voices
lulled me, and after a while I fell asleep.

When I awoke, the television was hissing its off-air sound.
I stumbled over to turn it off, and then I heard what had
roused me: the scratching, thumping noise at my bedroom
window.

I stood frozen in place, every nerve in my body sparking. A

few seconds passed. Then there was a shuffle on the front steps. The door latch clicked once, twice against its lock.

The decision I made then seemed no decision at all but automatic, instinctual. I turned and walked into my bedroom, where I took the 20-gauge from its rack. I opened the top drawer of my dresser, found the cardboard box of shells, then sat on the edge of my bed and loaded—four into the magazine, one into the chamber. The gun felt good in my hands, the stock sleek, the action and slide well oiled.

I rose and walked back into the living room, turning off lights as I went, the darkness falling in behind me until I reached the lamp by the couch. I stood for a moment, then turned the switch. I felt my way to the room's center, lowered myself to the carpet. Crossing my legs, I rested the gun on my knees, clicked off the safety, and waited.

The sounds became louder, more insistent. He was growing impatient, moving from the door to the kitchen window, from there to the bedroom, then back to the door. I followed his movement with my eyes closed, visualizing his steps from one entry to the next, feeling his growing frustration and then his fury as he hit the door hard, as he tore the screens from my windows.

But then it was quiet. He had given up, aware, perhaps, that the noise he was making might undo him. I opened my eyes and saw nothing but the familiar silhouettes of furniture.

How long had it lasted? Two minutes? Ten? Certainly, long enough for me to have dialed the emergency number in the front of my phone book, which still lay where the man had left it. But I didn't. How could I ask the police to defend me, defend a virtue I no longer possessed? I wasn't even sure I knew what rape was anymore. Somehow, whatever was happening was between me and this man, who wanted me so badly.

My legs were numb, and I stretched them out in front of me. I clicked on the safety. I pulled a cushion from the couch for a pillow, spread the afghan across my feet. Lying there, in the darkness of my apartment, listening to the sounds of distant traffic, I felt the rigidness ease. I slept that way, my gun beside me. I did not wake or dream that I can remember until the sun shone in my kitchen and I could hear the rasp of Mrs. Daniel's rake across the concrete edges of her garden.

IT WAS MRS. DANIELS who reported to the landlord what damage had been done. Not only had the aluminum screens been torn from my windows, but her flower bed had been trampled as well.

"You've got to call the police," she demanded, pointing at the large footprints that surrounded and crossed her lovely mums.

They sent a detective to my office at the insurance company. He smelled of fish sandwiches and coffee. I pushed aside the ledgers detailing the benefits of whole-life versus term to make room for the heavy album he unfolded, the pages of men who fit the description I'd given: medium build, dark hair, mustache. Some were dirty, faces scarred and pitted. Others looked pale but well mannered, like the shoe salesmen from my childhood who sold my mother our Buster Browns. Still, it wasn't hard to find the one whose features I'd studied that night in my kitchen, trying to place his eyes, his lips, his hair. My only surprise was that the name of his supposed friend—Bill Talkington—was actually his own.

"Why didn't you tell me?" I asked the detective, who finished scratching his notes and bound the folder tight.

"Best that you identify him by sight," he said. He blinked several times, cleaned the corners of his eyes with a spittled finger. He sighed, tapped his tired pencil. "You should know," he said, "that we suspect this man of other crimes."

"Then why did he use his real name?" I asked.

The officer stood, slid his chair against my desk. "That was a mistake on his part." He gathered his jacket, nodded his head. "This man," he said, "would not have expected you to live through the night. You will need surveillance until we can get something on him."

I felt impatient with the detective's smugness, his store of covert knowledge, the way his eyes settled on my knees, my wrists, but never my face. What other secrets did he shield? What topless bars and seedy back rooms had he visited? What fantasies swirled in his head, perhaps even now, as he straightened his belt and settled his change deeper in his pocket?

"What I need," I said to the officer, "is time to get my work done."

He looked at his hands—the unblemished fingers and two gold rings, the dark hair that tufted obscenely from beneath the cuffs of his shirt. "Call this number," he said, and left me with his card.

Chase, a young coworker bound for annuities and safe margins, stuck his head in the door.

"Everything all right?"

"It's okay," I said.

"Did you get his number?"

I looked at the detective's card, its stern lettering and gold emblem, then held it out to Chase.

"Here," I said. "He's all yours."

Chase's eyes brightened.

He didn't notice me gathering my briefcase, filling it with my nameplate, the few supplies I owned. By the next week, he would be thumbing through my Rolodex, adding to his accounts the clients whose files I left neatly alphabetized in the drawers of my desk.

WHEN DAVID RETURNED that evening, I showed him the jimmied windows and broken flowers. He kept his hands in his back pockets and nodded, kicked a few rocks.

"I should have shot the bastard," I said.

David looked at me, then smiled. "Maybe next time," he said, "it will be me."

I followed the movement of his hand, the cigarette brought to his lips, the way his eyes lidded themselves against the smoke. "What do you mean?" I asked.

"I've done it before. To old girlfriends." He inhaled deeply, ran his thumb and finger down the corners of his mouth. "Wait a few years, then hide behind the door, find a closet. They always fight at first, but they want it."

I stared at him longer than I should have—his hair unkempt, the tightness at his temples. "They know it's you," I said.

David dropped his cigarette to the gravel, crushed it with the toe of his boot. "No," he said. "They never know." He held my eyes for a moment, then shrugged. He turned, stepped back into my apartment, and I followed him, locking the door behind us.

That night, after David had gone, I looked from behind my curtains to see a patrol car parked across the street. Sometime before dawn, another came to take its place. Unable to sleep, I watched the spotlight penetrate my shades, trail the walls of my room. Each hour, as the false moon cast itself through my window, I pressed myself to the corner of my bed, as though I were the one they were seeking.

AT MY MOTHER'S ENCOURAGEMENT, I made plans to introduce David to my parents. David agreed to go but bristled when I urged him toward a nicer shirt, a less ragged pair of jeans. My father was in his recliner when we came through the door. I hadn't seen him for months. Nothing about him had changed. He wore a clean, Western-cut shirt, fresh jeans, white socks, no shoes. He had a pack of Winstons in his pocket and three or four toothpicks, a cigarette wedged in the V of his first two fingers. He nodded a terse greeting, then refocused on the television opposite his chair.

The air in that room could not have been colder. I was shaky with nervousness, with the gall it took to do what I was doing. My mother was, as always, civil. She had dressed nicely, as she did when welcoming company, and I was struck again by her youthful beauty as she busied herself between us, offering iced tea, a plate of saltines and Kraft Deluxe. She was as tense as I was, fearful of my father's reaction, knowing I was skittish and might fly again with the slightest provocation. My father furrowed his eyebrows, motioned at her with his two fingers. "Up and down, up and down," he said. "Why don't you just sit?"

While my mother and I made small talk, the two men smoked, wary and watchful, my father at least speaking, which I'd half expected him not to do. The conversation turned to trucking, common ground between my father and David, and now between my father and me. Was this yet another way I thought I might subsume my father's identity, become the projection of his interests and skills? Tandems and tons, torque and compression—I could hold my own, describe the stiff clutch beneath my foot, the machinations of backing a double-trailered tractor toward the narrow chute of a loading dock.

I could tell by the stiffness in my father's shoulders, the intentional aversion of his eyes, that even though he assented to join in the discussion, what my father felt for David went beyond simple indifference, beyond dislike. Beneath the patter of axles and engines ran a muted dialogue of embattlement. The unspoken umbrage I allowed myself in response to my father's taciturn criticism dovetailed with another emotion: whatever judgment my father lodged against David was a token of his residual devotion to me, the blood link between us.

Did David feel my concentration, my loyalties shift? He reminded my father that, as the supervisor for his trucking company, he had the power to hire and fire. He told my father that he should consider long-haul, to give him a call if he was interested. I understood, even then, the patronizing message such an offer invoked, and I felt the hair on my neck prickle. My father said nothing but blinked slowly. He would not allow himself to be so easily drawn in. Instead, he turned his attention to the television, leaving my mother and me to find a means of exit. I rose, shuttled the dishes to the kitchen, hesitated for a moment at the window, where the leaves of my mother's philodendron grew green and waxy along the sill. The lingering smell of sausage and fried eggs, the bleach-brightened cloth draped neatly over the faucet, the satisfying clack of drying laundry—for a moment, I felt the pull of familiarity, the deep draw of comfort and care.

I rinsed the crumbs from the plates, knew that I had taken all the time I could without raising suspicion. From where the plant grew thickest, I snapped a shoot no longer than my hand, rolled it into a delicate wreath, secreted it away in my jeans' pocket, then walked to where David waited at the door. I don't remember that my father rose from his chair or that my mother kissed me good-bye. I remember sitting next to David as we pulled from the driveway and feeling that I mustn't look back, that what lay before me was now of my own making. I could feel the downward course of it, but I could not admit such fault. Better to suffer the consequences than to become the prodigal daughter forever doomed to gratefulness and humility.

David and I rode in silence. He was tired, he said. He needed to sleep before hauling out that night. When he dropped me off at my apartment, I did not encourage him to stay but waved as he drove away. Inside, I filled a jelly glass with water, unfurled the limp shoot. I worried that it would not live, that even the short trip between houses had been too much, but when I awoke the next morning its leaves had plumped, and I believed that I could already see the white nubbins of roots forming along the stem. "*Anybody,*" my mother had often said, "can grow a philodendron." I would need a planter and some soil. I would trail it like ivy along the corners of my cupboards. I would polish the leaves until they shone.

A FEW WEEKS LATER I lay in the dark of the sleeper, listening to the wind that had forced us to pull off the road. The cab of the semi shuddered and bucked. We were miles between cities, somewhere in the desert of eastern Washington. David had turned off the engine to conserve fuel, and in the absence of our light the blackness seemed an ocean. We were floating, our world a four-by-six room of vinyl, metal, and glass pushed and pulled by deep currents.

I was frightened by the wind's intensity. I'd seen the trailers blown sideways, the loads tipped. I could feel the framework twist, the many wheels lift and settle. Tumbleweeds of sage scratched along the truck's underbelly; the windows whistled and moaned their sad news.

David sat behind the steering wheel. I wanted to touch him, wanted to feel the length of his body warming the cold mattress on which I lay. I wanted his words of comfort to calm me, and the only way I knew to ask for this was to caress and proffer, draw him to me with my hands and lips.

He ignored my imploring, pushed me away. He had to keep watch, he said, be ready to go the minute the storm lessened. But I knew it was more than this; he was angry in a way I had not seen before. I knew, too, what had brought about David's wrath: in Seattle we'd come to a heated disagreement over the next step of my initiation. I wasn't to the point he had hoped I would be, unwilling to allow the permanent markings he wanted to be placed upon me: the piercing rings and lasting tattoos, his rites of ownership, my rites of passage into the world he imagined for me. There were places on First Avenue, he said. Some of the work could be done there. My refusal was soft at first, then steady. "No," I'd said. "I'm not ready."

He had studied me for a moment, gauging my resolve. Perhaps he saw clearly what I, as of yet, could not: there were places I would not willingly go. I was beginning to see that what David offered had not brought me the kind of freedom I had anticipated. I was tired of dancing, tired of the loud music coming from David's tape player, his radio, the juke-boxes and bands in all the bars we entered. I no longer wanted to perform for David, and I had begun to understand that I could never perform for the men who gathered in the blue-lit clubs. In the truck-stop bathrooms, I locked myself in for long minutes, breathing in the smell of disinfectants, calmed by the white metal stalls and country music—Dolly and Merle singing me back home. I needed to get away, leave the parking lot with its lineup of trucks, but I could not imagine the steps I would take from that room with its stain-less steel walls scratched with names and numbers. And I would think, "I *can* leave if I really want to." And even now, I think, "He could have hurt me worse, but he chose not to. How can I condemn him for that?" What damage had I in-curred? What trauma did I hold as evidence? My face was not cut. My arms were not broken. Whatever lay in front of me was the projection of my own desire to know what I should not know, to feel what I was not meant to feel.

Through the last hours of the storm, I lay with my eyes open, hoping for light. When the sun finally rose up before us, a salmon medallion in the east, David pulled onto the highway, and we passed by the wheat fields and dairy farms, the schools with their bicycles all in a row, the town halls and neat cafés advertising their special of the day. We were joined by other trucks and cars, people headed to work, to coffee with friends, and in the face of such common things the nightmarish hours before seemed suddenly false.

BETWEEN US THEN THERE WAS SOMETHING not new, but newly recognized. It had always been there—that awareness David and I had of each other's strength, how we held so deeply to the belief that one would outlast the other. David had pared me down to the bone, to that point where I would offer up scapula and femur, pubis and spine, but not the marrow he wanted, the life core.

In the face of our battle, everything else fell away. Just as David had reduced me to my most basal self, his fervor to dominate had brought him to the zenith of his power. He no longer hid his ambition. I knew that while I filled the hours when he was away with *Star Trek* and paperback romance, he would do what he had told me he would do: find the women in Seattle who most pleased him.

I was not allowed jealousy or any other sense of possession. I stayed with him because I wanted to, he said, because what I wanted was not only him but every man like him and even the women that he lay with. I wanted them all around me, all at once, my bed full of mouths and teeth and tongues, didn't I?

No was a whisper I hardly remembered. What David demanded of me left me weak. I exhausted myself suppressing awareness. I must not hear, must not see myself as I was, powerless, unable to scream. And if I had been willing to call out, who would have heard me? It was too late, I knew. I'd gone too deep into the forest. I had only the night and its darkness and the hunger all around.

"Are you afraid?" David would ask, those times when I faltered, when I failed to do what he asked of me. I didn't know how to answer. "Yes," and he'd breathe in my fear and become more cruel. "No," and he'd smile because soon I would be, I must be afraid.

"THERE ARE SOME THINGS BETTER LEFT UNSAID," my mother has told me. I wonder what those things are. I wonder if somewhere in those untold stories I might have found a map of experience I could follow, some way to believe I was not alone in my confusion and misjudgments. What we fear most we bury deepest, so that the very thing we must detail manifests itself in abstraction: "Stay away from *that* kind of man." What kind? The kind that doesn't kiss you on the first date, doesn't maul you on the second? The kind that buys you flowers, makes good money, doesn't leave you with blackened eyes and a broken jaw?

We give what directions we can: *keep your nose clean, your chin up, your legs together, your mouth shut.* Yet, so often the truth lies in what we cannot say. Blind cartographers, tongue-tied guides, we send our children off with maps drawn in invisible ink, pointing down the Yellow Brick Road toward Oz without a word about flying monkeys.

Nothing about the bedside table, its drawer holding

scarves of various color, the weave of knots whose tying must be learned, intricate details, instructions passed on from one initiate to the next.

"*Like this,*" David whispered.

Like this.

THERE WAS RELIEF IN LEAVING BEHIND my life-insurance portfolios, the calculating of cost and benefit, worth and risk. I got on at the local drive-in, where the most demanding task was mastery of the milk-shake machine. What money I brought home paid for rent and little else. When it became clear that David's truck driver's salary could not keep up with his lease, the parties, and freeloading druggies, he cleaned out his apartment and moved in with me, bringing with him his guns, knives, and great horned owl, which he hung above the fireplace, its yellow glass eyes persistently fixed on some point just above my head.

And so, with our clothes in the same closet, our dishes and pots and pans nested in the same cabinets and drawers, I began to imagine a life with David, one that would redirect our course, offer us both good shelter. Perhaps I still believed what I'd been taught—that it is the woman who determines the character of the man, feminine virtue that tempers male vice: with our quiet selves we give comfort; with the infinite grave of our suffering, we swallow transgression. I would make for David the home he had never had, create for him a life to make up for his own fractured past. I would nurture him, keep him fed, his clothes laundered, his sheets clean. He would find more comfort in my bed than in the arms of dancers. He would learn to give love instead of pain. I'd mend the story, make it work. I'd focus on what we shared, what I believed had brought us together in the first place.

Like David, I was drawn to the romance of self-sustenance, of living on wild meat and native trout, frozen huckleberries, watercress picked from the wash of a mountain spring, morels sprung up beneath the northward shading of yellow pine. The few times we spoke of the future, it was in terms of isolation: how far into the country we'd like to settle, how far away from highways and quick-marts.

David's aging aunt lived in such a place, on a homestead near a small north Idaho town, where David had spent much of his boyhood, exploring the forest with his .22 rifle. In the late fall we went there to hunt elk. While the old woman told the old stories, frying bacon on the wood-fired cookstove drawn up the river sixty years before by a pair of mules on each bank, I peeled potatoes and thought of the lumpy little bed where I'd sleep that night, alone in deference to her aged authority.

The intimacy of early cold light is what I remember: rising to pull on my long johns and jeans, a jar of home-canned pheasant for breakfast, filling the Thermos with coffee and my pockets with shells and homemade jerky.

As David and I walked toward the crest of the mountain, I felt again that which I have always loved—the encompassing sanctuary of wilderness. Sunlight shot lacy and low through branches of Ponderosa pine. Tamarack lit the hillside, yellow beyond yellow against the dun of frost-killed whortleberry. What leaves of sumac remained had gone from blood red to black. We crossed through thick stands of Douglas fir, over the small streams that washed across rock and emerald moss. The smell of forest floor rose up wet and green, spiced with juniper and the hard red berries of kinnikinnick.

I followed David through the woods, felt the life come back to my arms and legs. This is what it could be like, I thought, if the rest of the world would fall away. I believed, simply and absolutely, that it was what was outside the wilderness that corrupted, believed it with the earnestness of my father when he was young.

Every few minutes I reached out and bent a limb of vine maple, raked a thumbnail of bark from a sapling. I scanned the horizon for landmarks—split-top firs, an exposed shoulder of rock. The day was clear, and I plotted the sun's course across the sky, relieved by its sure rise toward noon. When we stopped to listen, I dropped my jaw to quiet my breathing; bent down to press the small, round droppings of deer between my fingers, testing for warmth; raised my face to sniff the air for musk, the pungent odor of a urine-marked tree.

After hours of walking, we'd seen no sign of elk or deer. I slowed, let David lengthen the distance between us. As I leaned against a lightning-struck pine to catch my breath, I held my arms away from my sides to catch the breeze.

I've got to keep up, I thought, will my feet to go forward, my lungs to hold air. "You should be able to walk this kind of country all day"—my father's words. I felt a sudden longing for his presence, for his voice urging me farther along the trail. "It's all up here," he'd say, those times during the hunt when I stopped to rest. He'd tap his finger against his forehead. "If you think you're tired, then you're tired. If you think you ain't, then you ain't."

Always, this code of mind over matter, the belief that endurance has less to do with physical strength than a steely determination to overcome the body's inherent weakness. Such stoicism had split our family into those who would never be broken and those who already were. It was my father I aligned myself with, a man who could empty his mind and never feel the pain, who could, if he must, reinvent the word.

I closed my eyes, took a deep breath, caught the incense of David's tobacco mixed with yarrow and wild onion. I balanced the Winchester in the crook of my left arm, remembered all the times I had seen my father handle the rifle in just this way. I spread my fingers across the walnut stock, studied the shape of my knuckles and nails, so much like his. I touched the trigger, felt its light resistance, looked up to see David almost out of sight.

I'd nearly caught up when I saw him stop. I heard it too: the high whine of a voice rising to a scream. My skin prickled and I looked at David, who stood with his head cocked, gathering in the sound. Again the shrill howl echoed up the canyon. Not coyotes, I knew—it was too early in the day, the sound too human. But not human. Something else, moving in pain, in fear.

"Sounds like a bear," David said.

"Trapped?" I asked, then the scream rose again, more distant this time, farther down the draw. David shook his head and turned back to whatever invisible path we were following.

I shrugged the rifle onto my other shoulder, still bothered by the keening cry, worried about the suffering. We'd seen other hunters; a helicopter had flown over us, illegally transporting a roped and bundled bull elk, hanging down like a pendulous tongue. I thought of the army chopper David had shot from, felt the hair on my own neck rise as the rotors beat the air above us.

"It's no good," he said. The forest seemed full of noise and movement, cheating us of surprise. There was no silence, no isolation from the sounds of guns and motors. When David turned, I knew we were headed back toward the river, toward the house with its small beds and water pumped from the spring. It wasn't the sun that told me so, or the geography of trees and ridges; it wasn't anything I could name. I just knew—*that way*—and knew that it was right. But I did not trust it yet. I'd let David lead me down the ravines cutting into one another, the deer trails that wove through the woods. I watched the sky darken against itself in gradations of blue—indigo, navy, cobalt, true—the last light at our backs as we stepped from the forest into the clearing and walked the few feet into a home not our own, but one that took us in and, for that time, made of us who we might otherwise be.

THAT NIGHT David and I visited the only tavern for miles, a small wooden building with two tables, a counter bar, a jukebox. The sole patron present left a few minutes after we arrived, tipping his cap to me on the way out.

David knew the owner, a middle-aged man who introduced himself to me as Smith.

"Order what you want," said David. "Smith's a magician."

The tavern served beer and wine—no hard liquor without a license, which Smith didn't have, but he did have a locked closet. From it he drew David's Jack Daniels and the vodka and Kahlua he needed to mix my drink. He made me six Black

Russians during the course of the night, each heavily dosed, as I listened to the stories—the same stories I'd heard at other bars, around campfires, at the holiday table: the wealthy man from Texas who shot one of his hunting guide's mules; the politician from California who came girded with enough Weatherbys and Berettas to bring down every deer for miles, hit nothing, then offered a wad of bills for someone else's kill.

The talk of good families and bad years, when the snow got more than the hunters, years when all you had to do was step onto your back porch and pick your shot—I felt comforted by the men's words, the rhythm and reason of story. I had heard the same tales all my life, the cycle of seasons marked and defined by meat, the narratives passed from one generation to the next, in each telling the understood message that to be accepted inside the circle, you must *prove up*, survive with grace whatever weather, grief, or danger comes your way. You must, above all, take responsibility for your own failed doings. I never questioned the dictates of this code, and much of me still believes in its simple truths. I know, also, that such harsh judgment can silence those narratives whose telling might offer the comfort and continuity of shared experience. Without the truths that are lodged in every life's telling, the old narratives thin, become brittle, and shatter, and we are left in chaos, no trail to follow home.

By the time I staggered from my stool that night, I was singing along with Jimmy Buffett, "Wastin' away again in Margaritaville." We were nowhere near a Mexican sunset, but the liquor warmed me and I felt strangely at peace. We left the bar and stepped into the cold. The sharp smell of wood smoke, the stars so bright and distinct they made of the black sky a thing of light, the air itself an incense of cedar—

I shuddered with love for it, for the rush of knowing I belonged there. We drove the few miles back to the house, where David's aunt was already sleeping. I crawled into the narrow bed she had made for me, beneath quilts worn thin by the pull of hands.

In the next room I heard David cough, the rap of his bed against the wall between us. I felt a sudden yearning to touch him with tenderness, as a wife might, to rise in the morning made new by pure air and a desire born of love.

I believed in this possibility because I believed in redemption, in rebirth, because even though I had left the faith, there yet existed some faith that had not left me. I had felt the conversion that comes of spiritual and emotional purgation; I had seen how a drunk could stagger to the altar and walk away sober, how a mother could suffer the death of her child, kneel down and rise in peace. Souls saved, bodies healed, families mended, the blind made to see—I lay there, without prayer, without intercessor, yet still believing in that directive given by Saint Paul: "Be ye transformed by the renewing of your mind."

I imagined the miracle of a good life, the life that my father had dreamed of, how I could circle back and pick up the trail, follow the path back into the wilderness, return to that spot where the demon had found him, chart a new direction. I believed that if I could just stay in that house, where the stove huffed out its honest heat, stay in that clearing by the river and live by the codes of sustenance and provision, I would be happy. I could hunt with David, cook for him, pick fruit from the trees and seal it in jars, follow him across mountains and sleep in the meadows—be everything that my mother was, and everything that she was not.

I thought of the young boy David had once been, napping in this same bed perhaps, or playing outside in the barn, where one summer he helped his aunt raise an orphaned fawn. He still remembered the way it suckled, pulling at his fingers, the smooth leather of its mouth around the bottle's nipple. I had never seen the affection I heard in David's words, but it was there, somewhere, and I would, through my patience, my sacrifice, coax it from him.

Lying in the damp room, smelling wood smoke and the yeasty odor of bread dough rising near the stove, I realized that what I was feeling for David was something like love. I realized, too, how much I missed the calm and constant safety of family, how much I longed to re-create the circle that had once protected me.

At that moment I made a traitorous decision: no matter what David said, no matter how many other women he chose to bed, no matter what he believed he wanted and must have, I would no longer lie with other men. I whispered the promise to myself, felt a new determination. I gathered the blankets tighter, tucked my chin to keep in heat. Outside an owl made its silent sweep across the meadow; the voles scattered seeds in their burrows of grass. The deer came with their luminescent eyes and drank from the river, dipping their heads, offering themselves to the moon, then turned back to the narrow paths so that the sun might not find them on the open aits, vulnerable and exposed.

THE NEXT DAY, we learned from a neighbor that the howls we heard had come from a yearling bear, gut-shot and dragging its intestines across the forest floor. I can still hear its bawling, its distraction and pain filling the canyon like fire. I hear, too, the recorded cries of a dying rabbit, projected from the camouflaged tape player David used to call the coyotes in. I remember how we would rise from our blind and shoot the coyotes where they stood, looking our way, ears pricked forward, curious, nearly hopeful, then, at the last moment, sure.

DECEMBER 24, I LAY ON MY COUCH, trying to concentrate on whatever sitcom David was watching to keep my mind off of the pain wracking my stomach. A virus had left me weak-kneed and pathetic, sipping 7-Up instead of champagne.

The week before, my mother had called to invite me to the holiday dinner. Roast turkey, ham, mashed potatoes and gravy, sugared yams, chocolate pie.

"What about David?" I'd asked.

My mother sighed. "You know how we feel about him," she said. "Your dad wouldn't have it, even if I would."

How long had it been since I had seen her, my father, my grandmother or brother? My thoughts of them came to me like distant memories, images from a photograph: mouths frozen in silent smiles, eyes peering into the dark lens of my face.

Les and Marc stopped by with gifts that Christmas Eve. Les sometimes seemed the only tie left, the lone thread tethering me to my family. David devoted a great deal of attention to Les, invited her to the parties, plied her with dope. She met his interest with casual disregard, took what she wanted and left. I wondered if she knew the truth of my life, the stories that I could not tell her. I watched as she and Marc drank wine with David while I sat at the end of the couch, shivering with fever. I felt disoriented, as though I were separated from the others in the room, as though I were in a box of glass, cut off from their conversation and laughter.

When I rose to use the bathroom, I saw David avert his eyes, not wanting to see me still in my robe, my hair unwashed, my colorless face. I closed the door and rested my head against the tub's cool porcelain. My resolution of fidelity had not brought the reward I had hoped for. Instead of drawing us closer, my refusal to play the role of communal concubine had only served to alienate David. If what I longed for was deference and compassion, what I'd gained was neglect and isolation. "This is not *my way*," David had said, arguing that I was ruining what was good between us. If I thought I could change him, he said, I was wrong.

When I came back into the living room, Les and Marc were preparing to leave. As I slumped onto the couch, I saw in their eyes not just sympathy but something else: pity. I felt disgust for myself then. They had seen how David ignored me, had heard him say he'd be going out for the night. They may have wanted to gather me up and take me with them, feed me broth and sweet tea, but David stood between us, ushering them outside.

I closed my eyes and heard the door latch, then the sound of David dropping change into his pocket, the slide of his wallet against his hip. I pretended sleep when he walked past the couch, heard him hesitate for a moment at the door, then felt the cold rush of air from outside. When I opened my eyes, he was gone. Christmas lights flared against the frosted windows. I became aware of the songs coming over the FM station, songs of joy and celebration, God and angels, peace on earth and a star in the East. On the mantel beneath the owl, I'd pegged two of David's wool socks. I studied them for a while, wondering what I'd thought might appear in each, what bauble I might rise to Christmas morning.

I wanted the sickness to be over, and the holiday too. I wanted nothing more to remind me of how alone I was and how I'd chosen this path and had no one to blame but myself. "You made your bed, you lie in it," I whispered to myself. I looked at the owl, its outstretched wings so large they might cover me where I lay. I imagined the shadow of its body descending, the softness of its breast. I'd always loved the owls, suddenly there, looming white in the headlights, their solemn, monastic calling.

And then I realized I was angry, that the anger had been with me from the beginning, when I had first seen the owl and realized that David had shot it—not for food or even for money but because it came into his vision and he desired to possess it.

I thought of my father, whom I had never known to kill except for meat or protection, who came to the forest as though to worship. I remembered the story he had once told me of the rare white raven he'd seen while working in the woods. "I saw it there among the others," he said, his voice still reverent, "like a ghost. Only that once, and never again."

My father did not covet the raven, as some would have, because he understood, because he had taught me, that some things are sacred, that some things are gifts.

I studied the owl, as though there were secrets it might tell me. I thought of the nights it had flown through, the distant stars that guided its flight. I thought of my father that night the demon came, how it was nothing he could make sense of, how it frightened him. He quit believing in light, in the solid shapes of walls, and began walking through the dark as though it were day, knowing what he may or may not see a mere reflection of what he carried within himself—like memory, or sin.

Could he have known what journey lay before him? Did his vision warn him of our family's fragmentation, his daughter's rebellion, her desire to run and be lost and never be found? I wondered if he cared anymore, or if he simply believed my destiny already sealed, with nothing he could do but wait.

And what if my father had come for me there, where I lay on my couch, sick and exhausted? Would I have feared him, as I always had—feared him for all that he did not do but was capable of, as though in the repression of his rage lay the greatest threat of all? What if he had gathered me up in his arms and taken me home? I might have resisted him just as I had John, my pride and bitterness disallowing such rescue. Or maybe to have him come would have seemed such an act of uncompromised love that I would have welcomed his strength, his protection. I wanted to imagine the walls broken down between us, our mutual forgiveness, the coming days full of a new and tender awareness. I wanted to be only his daughter and not the daughter of Eve. But I knew that any freedom I might gain should I go back was only imaginary; the rules would still be the same, an exchange of one prison for another. Better that I suffer because of the choices I'd made than to have no choices at all.

———

THAT JANUARY the cold came down hard, busting pipes, icing the streets. The snow settled into the draws, the twilight turning the mountains deep blue. As David had predicted, the coyote pelts were good, seventy dollars for each hide brought in.

There is so little I remember from that winter, so few images I can recall. David came off the road high on bennies, unable to sleep. When I stood beside him in front of the bathroom mirror, I was startled by his wild hair and beard, his dilated pupils, his wrinkled clothes. I got out the iron and did what I could, what I'd been taught to do for a man: crease the sleeves, smooth the placket, give the collar some starch. It was my mother's map I followed now, what I did to impose order, to make sense of the course my life had taken—hot-water laundry, bleach-cleaned toilets, sheets snapped straight and folded tight around their mattress.

I remember the strange weakness that took hold of me: at work, my knees gave way as I stood over the deep-fat fryers; my hips locked, and I fell, momentarily paralyzed from the waist down. The doctors injected dye, took X rays, performed their small surgeries. They showed me fine bits of cartilage and bills I could not pay.

I remember the slick passage toward Seattle, the ice on Snoqualmie's summit, the big rigs jackknifing around us, and David not slowing but easing us through and up and over.

"You've got to keep power on the wheels," he said. "You just can't stop."

I wondered if I would ever be able to do the same, forestall the fear, be sure of my direction. I knew the route we traveled by heart now, the way the city looked at dawn just coming into its light, the bay with its mist rising like steam, gray for that time, and molten. In the motel I would lie awake next to David, unable to sleep in daylight or dark, listening to the freeway traffic. I would think of the sex shops and prostitutes, lap dancers and pimps. For so long, I had seen them as characters in a book, harmless, absurd, but now I was beginning to see the bruised thighs and lips, the needle tracks and empty vials. I saw the businessmen leave, tucking their shirts, straightening their ties, while inside the women squatted over their toilets and smoked, waiting for the next to arrive. They seemed never to sleep, seldom cried, but they spoke of their children and drank and dabbed another layer of makeup beneath their eyes. How could I have been so blind?

MY LIFE, it seemed, was falling away from me in great clumps: I had alienated my friends and family; when, after minor surgery on my knee, I didn't check in with my supervisor at the drive-in, he replaced me with someone less likely to miss her scheduled workdays. Suddenly, I had no money to buy food or gas, no money to make the payments on my car. I felt peeled, raw, and wounded, relieved when David offered to cover my share of the rent and groceries until I could find another job.

"You can owe me," he said. "Fifty percent." I agreed, though I knew my salary would never match his and wondered how he thought I might pay.

Those pieces of my life that had remained outside David's influence were now more tightly bundled. It was no longer my apartment but his, not my black-and-white atop the chest but his color TV. My bed had been knocked apart and put into storage; his, he said, was more comfortable. His dishes in the cupboards, his guns in the rack. I look back now and see how I was disappearing, one room at a time, but what I felt then was less fear than hope: I was seeing not dissolution but domesticity. Even as I watched all my icons of independence vanish, I believed that what came to replace them was better somehow, more mature, what I should expect if I wanted a man in my life. And I believed that I did. I believed that what I wanted was David, not as I had known him, but as I believed he might yet be with me as his inspiration.

Who of us, then, was the most desperate? For just as surely as David had built his prison around me, he immured himself to my keep. There was this fetter between us, this chain of servitude and responsibility. I cooked for him, cleaned, and laundered. I counted the days of his hauls across Washington. I curled my hair, put on lipstick, dressed in the outfits he favored, sat on the couch and awaited his return. None of it seemed to matter. Even our once lively conversations had become stilted, as though we had emptied ourselves into each other and now must face the limits of our ken. No more riddles, queries about origin, lessons on reading the trail. Only silence and its undercurrent of rage. Our hours together were spent watching TV, reading. At some point during the evening, he would shower, put on the clothes I had folded. And then he would leave.

Whenever I questioned David about his life away from me, he reacted with anger. He must have felt my pulling away, not from him, but from the life he had planned for me. The terms had always been clear. If I wanted him to stay, I would keep my mouth shut, do as he said.

If David's frustration drove him to sullenness, I responded with exaggerated regard, stroking, pacifying, just as I had seen my mother mollify, take heed. But even the offering of my body was no longer enough to move David. He tensed away from me in bed and would not speak, so that I lay in the dark, cut off from the sound of him, the feel of him, and because my existence had become dependent on his acknowledgment and approval, it was as though I were no longer visible. I was the air around him, the sheets' caress, the light falling in through the window. I felt my resolve weaken, the fear of rejection rise.

I remember the panic of it still—David's turn away from me, the shunning—although I now understand his intention: to bring me to yet another level of subjugation, to destroy whatever scrap of self-will I still possessed. In the face of such rejection, that vow I had made to myself while at his aunt's house, snugged beneath covers, verging on dreams, now seemed foolish and impossible. In desperation, I begged David to tell me what I could do to make him *see* me again. It was true: there had been things he wanted from me I would not give, had thought I could not give, but now I said yes, that there was nothing I would not do or give or let be done to me. I would obey. I was that kneeling girl, offering my life, my soul, every part of me to win salvation, to regain my patriarch's good grace. I had learned my lesson. *Please. Do not cast me out.*

David brought his eyes back to me then. His demands

were not of the coarse nature that I thought they would be. He asked only this: that I trust him completely. I must be patient and prove that I trusted him by my continued silent presence—even though he would not say my name or even look at me.

I cried and swore I would do these things. I huddled against him in the darkness of our bed, felt the thinness of his back and legs, the rigid curve of his spine. I closed my eyes so that I could not see his face turned away from me. I folded my hands between my knees so they would not be wanton, would not implore.

The next morning, he said that this is how it would be, that I must not question, never ask where he was going or when he would return, but must remain constant and wait.

I lowered my eyes, bowed my head. When the door had closed after him, I lay back down on the bed, believing myself unable to rise, to walk or even eat. In the empty room, in the tattered gray light of predawn, I thought of my mother in her worn robe beginning to make the coffee, fry the eggs; my father, whom she would awaken and feed, whose clothes she would have pressed and laid out so that he had only to slip them on to be dressed and ready; my brother still dreaming whatever dreams a good boy is given—the crack of bat against ball, the car he might someday own, the girl whose blond hair fills his fingers.

I thought of my grandmother, who would be awake, having slept the shallow sleep of the old—her lavender room, color of the flowers she loved, the lilacs that grew close by her door.

Unreachable, that room, those people. I could never ask

them to take me back, to accept me once again as their own. I had burned that bridge, and the gulf that stretched behind me could never be crossed.

DID I BELIEVE that I deserved this final subservience, dues owed for the years I had fought to control my own existence? Punishment, after all, was my familiar, my most expected return. I look back and see how the rhythms of my life have followed this pattern: rebellion, punishment, submission, and then the cycle repeating. I would strike out, expecting the reprisal, perhaps even bringing it on. Always, I had understood the gravity of my actions, and always I knew what my actions would bring: the belt across my bottom, the switch across my legs, the open hand, eventually, the groundings and loss of my already limited freedom, the threat of eternity in Hell. But the discipline and the warnings I had heard all my life had not had their desired effect. I seemed never to learn.

Could it have been, then, that even as David punished me, drove me toward what he believed might be my point of breaking, I was preparing myself for battle, protecting that part of myself that yet remained outside his control, some fragment I had thrown to the sky, where it floated above me, quiet and invisible?

Closed in behind locked doors and shaded windows, I drifted, aware only of the moments when I woke, then wished myself back into sleep. There were sounds outside that filtered in to me, traffic, the high laughter of children walking home from school, but the sounds were dreams and

I liked them that way, let them weave into the deafness of my slumber.

Escape, denial, depression—all of these, of course. But something else: I was resting, gathering my strength. When the loop of outside noise began to repeat itself, became something familiar, I realized I had slept through the beginnings and endings of several days.

I rolled to my side, let my eyes focus on the simple shapes, the complex shadows of the dresser, the closet, the floor. There was nothing in the room that might hurt me, nothing except the blade of my own shame, my weakness and despair.

Instead of dread, what I felt was a calm that I had never expected. Released from its constant vigil to defend, my mind had emptied itself, and what came back into me was a clarity so intense I could taste it, see its colors: icy and blue and deeply translucent, like the water come off the high mountains. As a child, I had mimicked my father as he knelt beside the spring's course, dipped his hand and drank. The cold had shocked my teeth to numbness, but when I raised my head, the trees were distinctly drawn, newly made, strokes of charcoal against the sun's unbearable brightness.

Is this what my father had been looking for all those years before, when he had gone into the shelter, denied his body its sustenance? *To see things more clearly*, he'd said. *To see what must be done.* All that he had taken with him on his journey had been pulled from that brook, filling enough jars to keep him alive for forty days and forty nights, until his blood ran pure as the snow-chilled water.

I remembered, on one of our last hunts together, how my

father had led my brother and me into the forest, marched us for hours along skidder trails, across the ridges and down the draws of the country he had logged for cedar. I'd been pleased to be in his company, believing we were making headway, working toward common ground. I meant to show him what I was made of, prove to him my stamina, demonstrate the accuracy of my eye. What came instead was the moment he had planned all along: Greg and I had not been paying attention, he said, had been depending on him for our sense of direction. There was a lesson we must learn. "Now," he said, pointing at me, "you will lead us out."

How could I? Walking the long miles in, I had noted only the lean of his back, the easy gait that carried him effortlessly over logs and through the thick buckbrush and vine maple. I had not marked the dog-legged red fir, slashed a V in the bark of pine, bled the carmine vein of wild plum. Clouds melded the sky to metal; there was no sun to guide my way.

We wandered for miles, my father pretending the role of meek and willing follower, while all the time I inwardly raged. Finally, as the pewter sky darkened to lead, I'd turned to him in defeat.

"I don't know where we are," I said. "I don't know which direction is right."

He'd only nodded, moved toward a log where we might all rest.

"You look down too much," he said. "You haven't been watching."

He pointed the ember of his cigarette toward the horizon. "You've got to see it all, forward, backward, sides. You get lost in here, it'll be a long time before someone finds you."

I'd lowered my eyes, ashamed, fearful that he might see what I was thinking: *You* could. *You* could find me.

"You won't always have the sun, or even stars. You have to make your own map. Memorize it." He rose, stretched the stiffness from his back. "Now," he said, "let's go home."

And we followed him, my brother and I, feeling his largeness before us, knowing we'd been lost and then found, each of us full of anger and gratitude, love and hate, and an awareness that wherever we walked in the world, we would carry this truth within us.

I lay in my bed and heard my father's voice and the voices of others come back to me—the same voices that had promised consequence and retribution, that had prophesied my harvest of pain. What the voices offered now was not condemnation but the harsh encouragement that was also my legacy, the rough prod that had boosted me up from the playground when the bully knocked me down, that had made me despise self-pity and believe that I could withstand anything with the sheer will of my body and mind. It was my grandmother's voice, pesky and absolute, jolting me from morning dreams because there were chores to be done, joshing me from bouts of poutiness with a chuck under the chin. "Possum, possum, 'coon, 'coon," she would chide, and I knew this meant that I was "puttin' on," like a possum "sulled up," only pretending injury. It was my father's voice, unmoving in the face of my announcement that I could not walk another yard, or stand another allergy shot, or produce the answer to yet another of his obstinate questions: "Yes," he'd say, "you *can*." And that was the end of it, and I would go and do what I thought I could not, and I would feel strong. It was my mother's voice, when, ill with fever, I had fainted in the hall-way. "Kim, what's the matter with you! You get up from there!" she'd demanded, enraged by her own fear. And because she believed that I could rise and walk, I did.

There was some of this yet in me, composed of a faith I could not unlearn and a peevish belief in my own survival— and something else: my inherent willingness to disobey. I had suffered the consequences of disaffirming the authority of the church and my father. I had been shunned and shamed, prayed for and denounced. Always, I believed, I could survive.

That one fragment of will I had kept hidden from David came back into me, lodged itself in my breast. I saw clearly that things could not continue this way, but I had little sense of how they might change. Before, my boyfriends and I had "broken up," given back class rings and sobbed our regrets for a night or two. But I knew I could not simply walk away from this. All I knew to do was confront, and that is what I planned, knowing that even as I rose from my bed and began gathering my clothes, I was risking something I could not name but recognized—the rage held deep, boiling, boiling.

I did not doubt that I could run from David. I did not doubt he would find me.

IT WAS DARK when I left the apartment. I breathed in the crisp evening air as I slid behind the steering wheel of my Capri and coaxed the engine to turn over. I'd driven little in the last several months, always a passenger beside David. The car itself had fallen into disrepair. I pumped the gas pedal, worked the clutch, then remembered the linkage was broken and I had no reverse, only first gear. Straight forward, then, across the lawn and onto pavement, ten miles an hour, the small car screaming its resistance. I'd already called Les, asked if I could borrow her Mustang to get me where I needed to go.

It wasn't until I got to Les and Marc's house that I realized the time: after midnight, and Marc had to rise for work by five. He came into the kitchen, shirtless and barefoot, listened as I explained my intent: to find David, force him to face me.

"Are you sure you want to do this?" Marc asked. I'm not certain how much he knew of the truth of my relationship with David—perhaps only enough to understand the danger. "Do you want me to go with you?"

I should have a man with me. I could see that's what he was thinking.

"No," I said. "Thanks." I wasn't sure what I was doing or why I was doing it, but I knew I wanted to do it alone.

They watched me pull away, standing on the porch and waving good-bye like worried parents. I turned onto Thain, swung east. In my mind there was a map I would follow, a logical progression from one point to another.

I drove by his mother's house first, looking for his pickup, then headed toward downtown, cruising parking lots along the way—the Strike and Spare, the Sidetrack, the Arbor, the Bull Room, where Charlene and I had once drunk every last drop of rum the bartender could pour, then down Normal Hill to Modern West, with its enormous dance floor and fancy-booted cowboys who knew how to put a shine on the two-step. I searched the littered alleys behind Curley's and Effie's and the Silver Dollar. I turned on the radio, then clicked it off, distracted by the music: I wanted nothing to interfere with what might lead me, what sounds I might catch coming in from the night. I rummaged through Les's ashtray for anything worth smoking, lit the stub of a Winston, and kept driving.

Colored lights flashed through the shuttered windows of the disco; I could hear the steady bass beat as I checked the lineup of cars. I recognized a number of the vehicles, including John's four-wheel-drive, and for a moment I felt the pull of the known and familiar, the safe passage his strength might offer. I idled past the entrance, turned left, and caught the one-way over the bridge across the Snake into Clarkston, Washington, where the bars stayed open longer and people came to end their nights.

Smitty's Barrel, Der Litten Haus, the Jade Lantern. The Red Shield was the last chance for liquor if you were headed west out of town, and it was there I found David's pickup. I threw the Mustang into park and nearly ran before catching myself. I had to remain calm.

I entered the restaurant, through which he'd walk to get from the bar to the parking lot. I was shaking and winded as I moved to the counter. People turned to look, then slid their eyes away. I didn't care that my hair and clothes were mussed, that I'd forgotten to put on lipstick or blush. The waitress kept her eyes lowered, busying herself with my flatware and water. I ordered a ham-and-cheese sandwich, suddenly ravenous for food. She didn't ask me if I wanted a drink but simply nodded when I ordered a double gin-and-tonic.

It would be a lie to say I wasn't afraid, because I was, afraid in an excited, fatal way. My choices were to run or to stay and fight, and the impulse to face my enemy made my pulse race; in the mirror behind the counter, my eyes reflected back deep blue, my pupils dark and dilated.

I felt the gin hit hard and welcome. My plate was in front of me when David came out of the bar and into the bright light of the restaurant. Another woman was with him. He saw me immediately and stiffened, then told her to wait outside.

We were two patrons at the counter then, David and I, a tall, painfully thin man with wild hair, towering over a young woman who looked as though she, too, might be crazy. The air around us must have filled with the animal smells of fear and rage, for he was angered beyond words by my disobedience. It was the first time I had seen in him such loss of control, the only time I had seen any outward show of passionate emotion, and this strengthened my courage, for some part of the sterile mechanism that drove him had broken down.

"You don't want to do this," he said. "You don't want to make me mad."

He wanted to hurt me, and if it had not been for the place of our confrontation—well lit, peopled by potential witnesses—my escape may not have been so easy.

I absorbed David's anger, met his eyes and would not look away.

"You fuck with me, Kim, and you'll regret it. You don't want to know what I'll do to you."

I was beyond that now, beyond caring. Others were watching us, and I saw the burly cook come from his kitchen, wiping grease on his white apron. David saw him, too, and backed slowly away from me, never taking his eyes off mine until he reached the door, which swung shut behind him in a rush of cold air.

Yes, I assured the cook, I was fine. No, the man wasn't bothering me. I pushed back the sandwich I hadn't touched, drank what was left of my gin. The waitress slipped the tab into her pocket. I nodded my thanks, turned, and walked out the door. I knew David was already gone, and maybe I knew it meant nothing.

The way back to my apartment was a straight shot across the river and down Main Street, a right on Twenty-first, up onto Thain, another right onto Eleventh. I stopped by Circle K, asked for a pack of Virginia Slims, though I only had half the change that it cost me. I told the clerk I was low on money, that I would drop off the remaining quarter the next morning. She shook her head, placed the cigarettes in my hand, patted my fingers.

"I'll catch you next time," she said, then turned to the three boys who had followed me in, mumbling their orders for chew.

The smoke was a good thing, filling my lungs, dulling the hunger. Back in the apartment, I emptied David's clothes into grocery sacks, threw his belongings out on the porch, the last thing the owl, which came down heavy in my arms and smelled of dust. I clicked my fingernails against its glass eyes, felt the dry roughness of its beak, imagined its push from my arms were it to come alive, take flight, disappear from the lights of the city.

I thought about the past summer, when David and I had gone into the woods to scout deer for the coming fall. The day had smelled of grasshoppers and licorice; the cicada hum of insects trilled the air. We'd been following an old skid road, mostly grown over, idling down an easy pitch in granny gear, when, from the dense brush to our left, a whitetail doe jumped onto the road, then bounded up and across the ditch and into the woods on the other side. Behind her came a late fawn, still wobbly on its delicately pointed hooves. The fawn froze in front of us, confused by the noise, the sudden absence of its mother. Its ears were translucent in the sun.

"Watch this," David said.

He opened his door quietly, stepped out, slid the rifle from its rack in the back window.

"Don't," I said. "Don't shoot it." It was out of season, too young, too small. There was no reason.

He smiled at me. "I'm just going to scare it, watch it run."

He leveled the barrel, clicked off the safety. I felt my pulse quicken, a shout rise in my throat. I had not wanted to see its fear, the terrified jolt of its body. The fawn stood still, unsure of its direction, turned its head toward us just as the rifle fired.

There was the shock of the noise, which I'd expected, but instead of scrambling for safety, the fawn had leapt up, then crumpled in a dervish of dust, its spine severed.

David looked from the fawn back to me, and I saw that he was genuinely surprised: David was an expert rifleman; he never missed his mark. He'd intended only to send the bullet under the deer's nose, encourage it to entertain us with its awkwardness and fear. It was the fawn's error, the fawn that had made the fatal move.

David scanned the road behind us for anyone who might have seen. He ran to where the fawn lay, picked it up by one thin leg, threw it high and far into the sumac and young lodgepole. I remembered the fawn's graceful flight through air, so golden and limber, the slow, undulate circles.

David would not meet my eyes. Had he felt it even then, my growing resistance to him? We had left that place, gone deeper into the woods, until David felt we were safe from detection, from any connection to the body of the fawn that someone might find while hunting squirrels or mending fence. The evidence would all be gone by now—the flesh eaten by coyotes, the joints separated and dragged and gnawed clean of the tender meat; the tufts of hair blown free, gathered by birds to darn their nests; the bones whittled by mice.

I stroked the owl's cool back, felt the dry quills beneath the satin feathers. I held it for a moment, then leaned it against the outside wall of my apartment, where it sat like a gargoyle, guardian between two worlds.

I THOUGHT I KNEW the dangers of opposing David. I believed I could bear the consequences. When he'd threatened me at the bar, I'd felt even stronger, more determined, and I knew that this is what I must do. I called his mother, said that he should come and get what was his.

The next day I watched as he carried the boxes and bags to his pickup. I didn't flinch, didn't offer a word of apology or regret. He came out of the bedroom with the shotgun John had given me, said he'd take it for what money I owed him— the rent, the food. He left me with less than he'd found me with, and that seemed right.

Why, then, having made such a clean break, did I call him

the next week, agree that he could come over for dinner? I know I was crazy with loneliness, but that is not enough to explain the risk I was taking. I can almost believe that I knew what it was, why it was *I* who must initiate some final scene: because he was not finished with me. I wanted control, owning what I could of time and place. If I called him to me, he could not take me by surprise.

Or was there part of him, part of who I was with him, that I could not let go of? Something more than simple dependence, something less than love—a last fix of the intoxicating rush of the forbidden he had introduced me to, a good-bye kiss to my bittersweet shadow.

I cannot cheat here; I do not mean to be coy. Let me play it like a movie, then, because that's how it exists for me, a reel that can be run forward and back and wraps around on itself and begins and ends and begins again.

A man comes to the door, and the woman lets him in. They talk, a few cool words, then she rises to make dinner. They sit together on a worn green sofa, plates of deer meat and potatoes balanced on their knees. They watch TV. We cannot hear the television or what few words pass between them. The woman drinks a single glass of the wine he has brought, but it goes to her head in a way she will remember later as odd, making her feel less drunk than pleasurably sleepy, a little giddy, high, really—the world seems a good place. He draws her to the carpeted floor, undresses her, ties her wrists and ankles, gags her with a scarf—the familiar gestures of his particular intimacy. He takes pictures with the Polaroid he has brought in a bag.

He hurts her then in ways he has not done before, and the pain and fear cut through the feeling she has had of floating, being coddled. She's quit fighting the ties that cross over her back and between her breasts because she knows how they are made to tighten this way. She tries to scream. Whether out of fear that a neighbor might hear or compassion she would never assume, he pauses, lifts her to the couch, unties her, takes the cloth from her mouth. But then he hurts her again. She cannot cry. She's tired, so tired.

He covers her with a blanket, wraps it behind her back. He's done with her now, she thinks. Now she can sleep. But then he lifts her and moves toward the door. Where are you taking me, she asks. There are others, he says, waiting. Others want to have her. He will take her to them.

No.

He hesitates in the doorway. There between the cold night and the warm room, she says it again. No. She says, I will scream. She says this without looking at him because she cannot open her eyes or raise her head, because she is so tired. She cannot be afraid because there is no fear left in her.

He stands in the doorway for a long time, it seems, holding her like a child, one arm beneath her shoulders, one arm beneath her knees. She rests, given over now to what must happen next, and when he turns and steps back into the room she is not surprised but indifferent.

He lays her on the couch. He kneels down beside her, strokes her hair. And then he tells her, makes this promise: just as he has done with other lovers, he will someday come back for her. Years from now, when she has nearly forgotten, when she is alone and the world sleeps deafly on, he will find her.

He leaves, closes the door behind him in a shush of air. She is asleep before the noise of his engine can reach her, and she does not hear him pull away. The woman, who as a child could numb herself to the belt, finds that she can once again shed her skin and slip away, untethered, untouched, dreaming of nothing, gone, gone, gone to the nothing-song of air.

13   *I LIE AMID A DREAMSCAPE OF ASH. The smoke comes to me damp and heavy, settles in my throat, my chest, my belly. I am trying to sleep, but the forest is burning, so close I can see its aura above the dark horizon. I rise from my child's bed and move to the open window, where I can watch the dome of sky—black, then melting to white, yellow, orange, red. I breathe in, taste the soot, almost sweet. I suck my finger, lift it to test the wind's direction. Hardly a wind at all, a breeze coming in from the west, but any movement of air might feed the fire and cause it to run.*

My father is there, where the red meets the earth, where the fire eats the trees and moves the air into funnels. He is swinging an axe, or running a saw, cutting what the fire would consume, stealing its hunger. He is gray with ash, the white and blue of his eyes alive in the blackness, and he is alone because that is how I imagine him, because he has said that he works best that way and thinks best that way—because that is how he makes sense of his life. I want it to be good for him, to be just as he wants it, so that he can fight the fire well and it will not hurt him.

In the kitchen, my mother works—the click click *of dish*

against dish. A pot simmers on the stove—brown beans fat with bacon. The table is set with plates and forks and knives, salt, butter, cornbread in its cast iron skillet covered with foil. There is tea in the refrigerator, cake in the oven. She has to keep busy, keep the food in its place, the dirt in its place, the children clean and fed and where they should be. She believes I am asleep, as my brother is in the room next to mine, and I think I should lie down and close my eyes, but then I can't breathe because the smoke is thicker with my eyes closed. I wish I could go to her, but I know she would scold me. It is late, and she, like my father, prefers to work alone, efficient in her chores, quick and precise.

The fire could shift, the wind rise up. The fire could crown, racing through the tops of the trees, a whirlwind of heat, impossible to outrun. The fire could find us, where we live in the hollow with the trees all around. We are circled by trees. I try to imagine our path of escape, what route we might take away from the fire, but there is nowhere for miles, nowhere without tinder and fuel. But my father would find us, I believe. He would lead us out. He is notching the tree with the fire in its crown, stepping back as the trunk begins its slow pivot and fall. The smoke and ash rise up and cover him. He is a ghost, wading the fog of cinder. Even his footprints swirl and disappear. He has gone where I cannot follow.

I remember what I have been told. Don't panic. If you run, you will die. But the berries I might eat are all gone, the spring choked with charred branches. The fish are dead, floating like pearly toy boats on the water's surface. Everywhere I look the forest is burning.

I squat and lay my head in the nest of my arms, my world a dream I'm adrift in, smoke and fire, dust devils and dry air, stench of burned flesh and birds crying. Somewhere, my mother is praying. The sound of my father's voice comes to me like a whisper.

I AWOKE still swaddled in the blanket with which David had covered me, the early sun coming in tilted and gray. I lay for a long time, trying at first to remember, then to forget.

I moved to the shower and stood beneath the hot spray, not thinking about David or food or money, not thinking about anything except how the water ran from the top of my head to my shoulders, back, and legs, then into the drain. I sat on the couch, smoked one cigarette, then another and another, until the pack was empty. Strips of thin light shone through the curtains, and when I stepped to the door and looked out, I saw the spring grasses and the trees suddenly green.

I felt a sudden, urgent need to get away from the apartment. I pulled on jeans and a sweatshirt, brushed my teeth, stepped onto the porch and stopped. I had no money. Les and Marc had retrieved the Mustang while I slept; my Capri remained in their driveway, only days away from repossession. I couldn't remember what time it was, whether it was Wednesday or Sunday, whether people were at church or school or work. I looked up the street, then down, began walking straight ahead, southwest toward the airport, toward the canyon where the Snake River eddied and slowed.

Four blocks, then four more. I turned east, circled back, exhausted. My mouth and throat were dry. Back in my apartment, I bent over the kitchen sink and drank from the faucet, remembering the cool splash of spring water on my face. I knelt, rested my head against the cupboard door, then lay down on the kitchen floor, and the sleep came again and there was nowhere I must go.

A WEEK LATER, when the landlord knocked on my door, he could not meet my eyes, and I saw in his face my own shame reflected. The rent remained unpaid: I had ten days to pack my things and leave. I ate what little was left in my cupboards, then scavenged aluminum cans from Dumpsters, pawned the thin gold ring that Tom had given me with his promise of love. I bought white bread, canned chili, cigarettes, cheap schnapps, its peppermint flavor a comfort, like the gum my grandmother passed to me in church when, as a child, I became restless with the everlasting Sunday sermon. That need I'd felt then—to escape, to make for the aisle and run for open air, to twirl and fall down in grass and watch as the sky continued its motion—still possessed me, but now without end, without the Amen of prayer, without the rising to stand, the being led away by the hand, away to the table set with fried chicken, string beans, white gravy and potatoes, corn from the summer garden, plums picked sweet from the shadowing trees.

I WILL ALWAYS BE GRATEFUL for the miraculous offer that came from Michelle, an acquaintance from high school, who had heard that I needed a place to stay and invited me to share a house with her and another roommate, Connie— both former cheerleaders, both students at the local college.

Although I had seen them little since graduation, I had known them for some time, having met them in ninth grade, after I had been expelled from my old school for truancy, after the summer spent with the preacher's family, when I had come to my new junior high fresh and eager. I was no longer the delinquent but a true crusader, bent on bringing every classmate to Christ.

Connie and Michelle had been easy targets for conversion. Both had sampled various religions with little sense of fidelity. Both had been involved in Girl Scouts and any number of other organizations, and they understood the ritual of presentation and gesture. But they had not cut their spiritual teeth on the pews as I had, and so their entrance into and exit out of salvation seemed comparatively unencumbered, as though they had simply outgrown Girl Scouts and were headed for Ladies of the Elks.

Connie had shoulder-length auburn hair that never lost its summer highlights, brown Cleopatra eyes that looked lined in kohl. Michelle was several inches taller. She had brown hair cut short, a long neck, large green eyes, a look that radiated disdain and froze men on the spot. Her mother had been a French war bride, and this seemed reason enough for her exotic beauty and seeming aloofness.

They helped me move my things the few blocks from the apartment to their house, made room alongside the pots of violets and shamrocks for my philodendron, which had begun to sprout runners and would soon grow a variegated border around the kitchen window. As I watched my new roommates laugh and cut up, jostling each other in the hallways, I felt the distance between us, the years, it seemed, that separated us from one another. Had I ever been like them? Even my skin felt old, my eyes and mouth used up. I could not imagine their interest in me, except to take up the spare bedroom and add another fifty dollars a month toward the rent, which they hoped I would do as soon as I got a job. I hung my clothes in the closet of my new bedroom, stacked my books in milk crates, nailed my rifle rack on the wall and underneath tacked my medals for marksmanship and my certificates in karate—hex signs, hedges against what haunted me. After the bars closed, I could feel safe with Michelle and Connie at TJ's Pantry, where we ate eggs and hash browns at three in the morning.

Lewiston is the kind of town that holds on to its generations. As I eased back into the normal flow of everyday life, I sometimes felt overwhelmed by the attention of old schoolmates who called my name across the produce aisle, or the parents who stopped me in the parking lot to show me photos of their latest grandchild. Often I averted my eyes, walked the other way, shamed and reluctant to construct plausible alibis about the years since graduation. Even in the company of women whose lives were directed by the normal desires and concerns of young adulthood, in the rooms filled with nothing more than the cast-off blouses and jeans of fashion indecision, I could not forget my life with David. What I wanted was to sit with someone, to talk, to be included in a circle that kept what was *out there* away. *Out there*—that place I had been so eager to gain, that wilderness of sight and sound, taste and touch, where I believed I might find some truer sense of myself. Perhaps I had.

Michelle and Connie never asked about my life before, and I offered little: it was easier to act as though it had never happened. And even if I had been willing to talk about it, what would I have said? What did I want them to know? I wanted to believe that in their innocence, I could find some remnant of my own. I slept with my bedroom door open to let the sounds of their breathing reach me, the small sighs of their dreaming.

There were times when I came upon David, at the gas station or department store, and he would smile at me knowingly and nod, and I would feel all the fear and confusion come flooding back. Shouldn't I hate him? Shouldn't I act as though he were a villain, a rapist, a thief? No. Because I believed it was not David but I who had brought it all on, and I believed he knew this and was secure in his knowledge, while I stumbled and flushed and hurried away.

The Polaroid photographs that he had taken tormented me. When I imagined what use they were to him, I felt a hot rush of humiliation. I did not want them in his possession, or in the hands of anyone he might show or give them to. I didn't think of this in terms of exposure; my fear was not that they would show up in some skin magazine. What I couldn't bear was the thought of them being passed from hand to hand, the moist fingers, the wander of eyes across my skin. I wanted them back, not because they were mine but because they were *me*.

I chose a night I knew David would be in town, pulled on black pants and black sweater, borrowed Michelle's car, and set out to find him. I'd heard he still didn't have a place of his own, and I knew that most of what he owned would be stowed in his pickup. Again, I cruised his mother's house, and then the bars, even the homes of some of the women I knew he most favored. I made my way across the Clearwater River to North Lewiston, circled around behind the motels and gas stations, and came upon a clutch of trailer houses, settling into their flimsy foundations, irises bunched tight in flower beds gone to grass. It was where one of David's fellow drivers lived, where we'd stopped once or twice for a beer.

David's four-wheel-drive was there. I turned off my headlights and coasted to a stop a block away, let the car door swing shut without latching. When I reached the driveway, I stopped to breathe before opening the passenger door of the pickup, switching off the overhead. I found them in the glove compartment, banded together in a manila envelope. I slid to the ground in a crouch, hurried to my car, and pulled away with my lights off, nearly deaf with the hot fear in my ears.

Back in my room, I studied the woman in the Polaroids. I examined her in pieces until she was no one I recognized, just arms and legs and hair and eyes. Then I took newspaper and matches and went out on the back patio, where I first lit my cigarette, then the pile of paper. I watched the pictures burn, watched the flesh pucker and bubble into ash, soft and still formed. I took a fist-sized rock and scraped and hammered until all that remained was a smear of black that the next good rain would wash clean.

PURGATION IS NEVER SO EASY. I don't remember when the nightmares began, but they came to me sure as sleep. I was being chased—someone meant to kill me. Most often, it was a man who hunted me, and I would wait in the shadows of a door or alley, hiding, preparing myself to strike for the eyes, the windpipe, to catch the knife blade brought down on me with the open palm of my hand, as the sensei had taught—allowing the piercing of flesh to avoid greater harm, wresting the weapon away.

I'd awaken, charged with adrenaline. Once, beset by near-panic, I reached for the telephone, dialed my parents' number. My father was working. When I heard my mother's drowsy voice, I whispered, "Please help me. I am so afraid."

My mother had never known me like this. She said, "You stay where you are. I'll send your brother."

It had been months since I'd seen Greg. He'd graduated from high school and was working in the pea fields, earning money to pay for college in the fall. He drove the few blocks to where I lived, pulled into the yard with his lights still on. He called to me from outside the locked door. I pulled on jeans, a shirt, let him lead me to his car. I was grateful for my father's absence, for the presence of my mother, who held me until the shaking and crying stopped. She made me a bed on the couch, covered me with the old quilts, stayed there, sitting at my shoulder, her hand on my forehead, quietly praying.

That night, for those few hours, I let myself come back into that circle of comfort, let myself be rocked and protected, let myself believe I was safe. But it was a belief that the light would not hold, and when the sky began to color, my mother and brother still sleeping, my father still driving the moon-licked highways, I felt the wrongness of my presence there. To stay would be giving in to that other life I no longer believed, the life from which I had made my first escape.

I pulled back the covers, heard my brother groan in the next room. My house was only blocks away. I would walk. I thought of my mother, how she would wake and find me gone. What did she make of my nightmare, my fear? She had lain her hands upon me, prayed that Satan take his demons and leave me in peace, and I wondered what demons she spoke of: the ones whose apparitions had filled my dream, or the ones she must believe still possessed me, drove me to reject the love she and her god might offer?

When I stepped out into the yard, I felt the chill of wet grass beneath my feet. In the east, the sun was a lavender promise. The streetlights dimmed and flickered off. I stood there longer than I should have, without coat or shoes, knowing my father would be coming home soon. I did not want him to find me shivering on his doorstep, lost and afraid.

I turned, opened the door behind me. Back to my place on the couch, where I could be warm for a while longer, where I could feign sleep and listen to the known voices whispering around me, until my mother and brother left for work and my father found his bed. Then, I would take a few pieces of the bacon they had left, borrow a coat, a pair of my mother's shoes. I'd leave that house and step back out into the city, its numbered streets and named avenues, where everything was familiar, where nothing was the same.

AT THE EMPLOYMENT OFFICE I sat listening to the sharp-faced woman behind the desk tell me how little was available for someone without a college degree, how my few office skills were not in demand, how, as a woman, I didn't qualify for the jobs that required heavy lifting. In my hand I held the letter stating that my pitch for unemployment benefits had been denied. She straightened her papers, making little taps with the balls of her fingers around the edges. If only I hadn't quit the bank, ditched the insurance company, she said, disappeared from the drive-in. So few points to rec-ommend me. I thought I might explain, speak of mistakes and regrets, but it all came out sounding like lies and excuses. She nodded without meeting my eyes.

I watched the decided way she separated my copies of the papers from hers, pushed them toward me. She smelled like baby powder. I stood, brushed the wrinkles from my skirt. "I'm a good worker," I said. "I learn fast."

She smiled tightly. "You might try the County Health Department for any medical needs. They charge minimal fees." She folded her hands atop her desk, said, "There are others waiting behind you." We were separated from the lobby by a low partition. I turned to see the line of men and some women, impatient and weary, a few dressed neatly, many wearing the ill-fitting donations of better folk.

No openings at the mill or bullet factory; nothing at Penney's or Sears. When I did apply for advertised posi-tions—at the offices and warehouses, fast-food chains and clothing boutiques—the response was the same: I'd been fired from my last job; my former supervisors would not rec-ommend me. I left each interview with less hope, less reason to spend my hours filling out forms and waiting for calls that never came.

When I went to the health clinic for free birth control pills, the nurse pointed at the waiting room. "You see all those women in there?" I looked from one young mother to the next, each carrying or scolding or ignoring a clutch of children. "You make sure you take these," she said, handing me the small plastic case. "You find work. You scrub floors if you have to."

SLOANE SUPPLY. The dress I wore to the interview had
long sleeves, hem to the knees, a modest neckline—and still
the middle-aged owner asked his few questions without taking his eyes from my breasts. When he offered me the secretarial position, I rose to shake his hand, but instead of taking
it, he looked at my open palm and grinned. Stupid, I thought,
for me to have risen first, to have stuck out my hand like a
man.

"See you at nine tomorrow," he said, and nodded that I
was free to go.

When I told Connie and Michelle, we celebrated. Money
to pay my share of the phone bill; money to buy new clothes,
get my hair permed, pay for breakfast at TJ's. Money to put
down on a used car. I felt hopeful for the first time in months.

Michelle dropped me off the next morning. Sloane Supply
was located in a refurbished 1950s house. The former living
room was now the front office, and as Mr. Sloane showed me
to my desk, I marveled at the sudden turn my life had taken:
a new IBM Correcting Selectric; a rolling office chair; a mul-
tiline telephone with a spongy shoulder rest; an electric pencil sharpener. The office skills I had excelled at while in high
school under the tutelage of Mrs. Morris—a stout, disci-
plined woman who wore black cat-eye glasses and believed
secretarial work was an exact science—were still fresh, and I
imagined the dictation I would take in shorthand, the speed
with which I'd add up the day's numbers on the ten-key. This
was my chance to do it right, and as Mr. Sloane leaned over
my shoulder to demonstrate the intercom, I was already lec-

turing myself on things to avoid: tardiness, daydreaming, misfiling, coffee left too long in the pot.

Mr. Sloane straightened. "It'll just be the two of us here," he said. "I'm in the back office. If you need anything, let me know."

I returned his smile and nodded. His dark hair was thick, left long over the ears in the style of a younger man. He had a pudgy look about him, a softness, as though water had been pumped beneath his skin and left to find its own level.

The minute I heard his door shut, I jumped to attend to the percolator, whose wheezing indicated the coffee was ready. I stood in the hall for a moment, peering into the other rooms, empty except for a few tables and rolled sheets of paper. I picked up the phone, listened to the dial tone, then placed it back in its cradle. I pulled out the desk's top drawer, which held a single pencil and three paper clips. The other drawers held nothing. I switched on the Selectric: the little metal ball made a satisfying whir and chatter. I turned to face the plateglass window looking out over Hillcrest Road and realized that I had absolutely nothing to do.

No files to put away. No typing or correspondence. Not a word on the Dictaphone machine. I opened the top drawer and separated the paper clips into compartments. I found a box of Kleenex and dusted the leaves of the philodendron whose vines drooped anemically down the sides of the file cabinet. I checked the few folders the cabinet held, making sure they were alphabetized correctly. I sharpened my pencil to a fine point.

At noon Mr. Sloane opened the door to his office. I'd fallen into a traffic-induced stupor, staring out the front window, and I hastened to make of my props what I could: the pencil across the desk pad, the phone's cord neatly spiraled, the phone itself at the perfect angle for retrieval.

He sauntered across the room to the window, hands in his pockets. "Plans for lunch?"

"No, I . . . home, I guess."

"You don't have a car."

"It's not far. I'll walk."

He turned and looked at me. "In your high heels?" He moved to sit casually on a corner of my desk, crossed his hands on his thigh, and leaned forward just enough for me to catch the smell of whiskey. "Aren't you hungry?" He leaned in closer. "Hey," he said. "Don't be surprised if your boss wants to lay you."

He winked, slid from the desk, and left.

I was stunned, less by the statement than by the suddenness of its revelation. He'd seen something in my face, in the way I had lowered my eyes.

I don't remember what I did for lunch, where I went, if anywhere. I waited. When he returned, he offered only a nod my way before closing himself in his office. From one o'clock until five, I did not move from my chair. The phone didn't ring. The only noises other than the traffic were the squeaks and shuffles Mr. Sloane made as he shuttled between the back rooms. At five exactly I rose and rinsed the coffeepot. I stood several feet away from his door and announced I would be going.

"See you in the morning," he called back, and in his voice I heard nothing that indicated threat or lechery.

I walked the six blocks home, wincing at the rawness of my heels, unwilling to take the shoes off and ruin my one pair of panty hose. I told my roommates that I'd get paid in two weeks, soon enough to meet the month's ledger of bills. I don't remember that I shared with them what had really happened, thinking that to do so would only enhance the view I believed they had of me as flighty, irresponsible, a woman who did not know how to comport herself around men in a nonsexual way.

It was like a scent on me—the smell of something clandestine, intimate, provocative. No matter how many hot baths and steaming showers, no matter the careful application of sprays and powders, no matter how long the hemline or loose the skirt, something remained to betray me. The next day's dress would be even more modest, the fabric heavier, brown instead of mint green. I rubbed ointment into my blistered heels, set the alarm, convinced by such small, domestic tasks that I could be dependable, become an older version of that sturdy working girl I had been only a year before.

I had begun to suspect that morality might lie in the exact and complete fulfillment of minutes and minutiae, a rigidly timed and compartmentalized existence. I would give myself no more than an hour for bath, hair, and makeup. I would eat one piece of toast, drink one cup of tea with only a teaspoon of sugar. I would borrow my roommate's sneakers and allow extra time for the walk to work, arriving at five minutes before nine. I would remake myself into that young woman others would be happy to see: content, temperate, and clean.

"HOW WOULD YOU LIKE TO GO TO HAWAII?"

Mr. Sloane stood in front of the plateglass window, hands in the pockets of his finely pressed trousers. He seemed enormously pleased with himself.

"Hawaii?"

"There's a conference. I thought you might enjoy it. You can take notes."

It was my second day on the job. All I had hoped for was steady income, a way to support myself; suddenly, I was being offered free travel to an exotic island, a stay at the nicest of Waikiki hotels. I could see by the set of his mouth, the slight smile, that he believed I could not resist his lavish proposal. A sudden, intense disgust replaced my apprehension, not because he had insulted my virtue, but because he believed me so naïve. I was no longer that girl David had discovered, no longer so easily wooed. Nor was I David's creation, although I could not yet say what shape my life was taking. All I knew was that I wanted nothing to do with this man or any others like him. I would starve on the street, I thought, before allowing such hands to touch me again.

I leveled my gaze. "What would your wife think?" I asked.

He pulled his hands from his pockets. His smile dropped to a straight line. "Mrs. Sloane," he said, stepping slowly to my desk, "is none of your business."

He left, went into his office, slammed his door. I took a deep breath, closed my eyes. When I opened them again, the world was framed in a four-by-five picture window, busy with the traffic of neighborhood people.

I rose and made my way to the empty coffeepot. A spasm of nausea knotted my stomach when I opened the Folgers: during the long rides I had taken as a child up and down the river road from the logging camps to Lewiston, I had often settled my chin onto the lip of an empty coffee can, the sickness of sixty-mile-an-hour corners unchecked by saltines.

As the water began to boil through, I heard Mr. Sloane's

door open. In the second it took me to turn, he had closed the distance between us. I took a small, sideways step, and he moved with me. I don't remember the look on his face or what he smelled like or the feel of his hands. I remember the coffeemaker's asthmatic breathing and the cramped muscle my body became as he pressed me to the wall.

I didn't panic or run—I knew too much about the excitement of the chase to do that—and I also knew that though I feared his strength, I would not go down without a fight.

"You don't want to do this," I said. Perhaps it was the cold resolve in my voice that caused him to pull back. I said, "Don't you touch me again." The look on his face changed from rapaciousness to rage. I watched him smooth his hair, and then he turned away, stepped back into his office, and closed the door.

The shaking came on then. I had felt it before, and I hated it. I worked my way along the wall, back to my desk, where I took off my high heels and began slowly lacing the sneakers. I'd have been surprised had he let me go that easily, and when his door swung open, hard enough to hit the wall, I straightened and waited.

He came toward me, furious, nearly wild. I stood my ground, set my eyes against his, saw how he stopped, pulled himself back into the shape of a middle-aged man, a wife at home, two children, a business to run. He blinked hard.

"I'm afraid I'm going to have to let you go."

I nodded and returned to the task of tying my shoes.

"Your work is inefficient. You are not self-motivated and cannot be trusted to see what needs to be done."

I picked up my purse and high heels. He pulled a wallet from his suit coat and wrote out a check for one hundred dollars. "Good luck finding another job."

The check floated at the tips of his fingers. I took it and walked out into the bright light that knocked the color from everything. For a moment I forgot which way I should go. I couldn't remember where I was at all. Then the colors settled back into the trees, the bleached asphalt soaked up its black ash, and I thought the day was good because of it.

I took the check Sloane had given me and stuck it in the frame of my bedroom mirror—it would cover rent and my part of the utilities, with a little left over. Maybe we'd go to the disco. I'd buy.

It would be several hours before Michelle and Connie got home from class. I lay on my bed, surrounded by my guns, my marksmanship medals, my karate certificates, library books piled high on the nightstand, at the bottom a copy of Marilyn French's *The Women's Room*. I did not yet know how this book would give me my first true taste of political awareness, how it would make me see my own struggle in larger terms, give me membership in a common sisterhood. I did not know that within months, I would be doing what the health-clinic nurse had urged, cleaning toilets and mopping floors before and after class, scraping together enough money to pay my way through college, into that larger world I had always longed for and nearly forgotten.

I picked up the novel I had begun the night before, found my place, turned the pages, felt my anger and frustration slip away. The night opened before me, the ways I could fill it without end.

WHEN DAVID CAME FOR ME the last time, he arrived midday and did not try to hide himself but appeared as a suitor might, an old friend. I don't remember that I thought to turn him away, not even for a moment. If I resisted this time, I knew that there would be another.

I sat on the mattress's edge and undressed as he watched, following the familiar routine. But something had changed. He could no longer reach that part of me that had once tensed beneath his hand. He had taken of me what he could; there was nothing he could do to resurrect some remnant of that girl I had once been, the woman he had worked so carefully to gain, to teach. What he had wanted was my willing trust, but *trust* was a word that now meant nothing to me. I observed myself from a distance, pleased by how little I was feeling, how great was my control: no emotion, no physical response. In this, there was power. I might never have to be afraid again.

It was a simple act between us, then, common and homely: I, as though the lumpish wife-servant, giving herself to duty; he, the coarse husband, taking his pleasure, taking his due. When it was over, I watched him dress, listened to the sound of his pickup grow more distant, and I knew he would not return, and that if he did, I would not know him.

I gathered my clothes, felt the seep of him between my legs, and this was the first time, for always before he had remained unfinished. In the beginning, I had thought this a sign of his control, his selflessness, his willingness to give and give without taking. Over time, I had come to see how it was he could not let go, could not allow that second's death to make him vulnerable, unwary. It was like an illness with him, a disease, and if at first I had wondered what it might take to bring him to that moment of completion, I had come to fear what it might necessitate, where it might lead.

Curious that it would happen now, as though the seed he spilled were emptied into nothing so different as his fist.

I cleaned myself with delicate rags. I found my book and cigarettes and took them out onto the porch, where I would wait for my roommates to come home. I lifted my face to the air, smelled the rain moving in from the south. I closed my eyes and breathed in the smoke, holding it as long as I could, until my skin tingled. I'd never felt so free.

I REMEMBER THE SPRING OF 1980, AN afternoon of May sunshine. The doors were open, birdsong and the smell of locust blossom dispelling the last rumors of winter. Michelle dozed on the couch, while I nodded over the texts I meant to study: *Child Psychology,* Erskine Caldwell's *Tobacco Road,* Ken Kesey's *One Flew Over the Cuckoo's Nest, Physical Geology.*

There is a sweetness to this memory because it is the beginning of what will become my new life. After months without direction, I had filled out the one-page application to the local four-year school, Lewis-Clark State College. There, through the grace of Pell Grants and government loans, I had begun my work toward a degree.

I'd opted for geology over algebra: as a child, I'd collected jasper and pyrite from the local rock shop, intrigued by the homely thunder-eggs with their secret vaults of crystal. Our professor, a compact man with white hair and mustache who smoked a pipe while lecturing, promised us experiments and field trips. He said we'd come to learn the difference between aggregates and achondrites, feldspar and shale. I loved the names, the sounds they made: smoky quartz, yellow wulfen-

ite, Pele's hair. And the maps—the measured contours, the
calculated distance. I understood the logic of creation and
negation—the buckle and shift, continental drift, the core of
iron and nickel, the cool outer core of molten metal, warm
rocky mantle, thin cool crust. The faults and layers, the rup-
tures, the ancient heave of lava—once thought to be the spill
of immortal anger, our professor said, now predictable,
nearly done.

Michelle and I must have noticed the sky darkening at the
same moment, for we both bolted for the clothesline to save
our towels and sheets from the impending storm. The bank
of clouds was moving in from the west, black with the
promise of lightning and bone-jarring thunder. I'd never
seen such a solid, dark mass, cutting the sky in half.

I was thrilled. I loved the change a storm brought with
it—the sense of being safely sheltered while trees snapped
and the booming concussion rolled off the mountains. I noticed the absence of wind, although it often happened like
this: one moment the air gone breathlessly still, the next moment, a howl of dust. I waited for the rumble of first thunder, but what I heard instead was the barking of dogs,
beginning somewhere distant, taken up a block at a time,
moving up from the valley bottoms until it touched the ears
of our neighbor's large mutt, who sent up a wail of recognition.

We threw the laundry on the couch, then stood at the open
door. We, too, felt it: something not quite right, a shift in the
known and expected. A few houses down, the crazy lady's
chickens made for the henhouse; the robins left their worm
beds to gather in the poplars and preen dust from their
wings. I knew that animals could sense tragedy, impending

disaster; I'd heard such stories from my grandmother—the chained hounds baying for days after the death of my grandfather, the fowl and beasts of burden given the power of speech at the moment of Christ's birth. Watch the cows: if they lie down in the field, rain is coming. Watch the horses: if they skitter and jump for no reason, there's a fire racing the field miles away, hail coming to beat the roof down. I thought of these things as the chorus of dogs rose and fell, then rose again, a warning or lament, I couldn't tell which.

Street lamps flickered on. The dogs stopped their howling. And then the ash began to fall. We thought it snow at first, stepped out and caught it in our palms, rubbed it between our fingers like moth wings.

I can't remember how long the darkness lingered, how long it took for the main body of ash to pass over our town, but it seemed only an hour, maybe less. The light came back slowly. The birds chattered. The roosters, fooled by the false morning, crowed hoarsely, buoys in the dry fog.

Back in the house, our soap opera had been interrupted by the Emergency Broadcast System. Mount St. Helens was exploding four hundred miles away. Michelle and I watched the news flash in wonder. Of all the things we'd been warned of in our lives, no one had ever mentioned volcanoes.

If you know what to look for, you can still see windrows of it along the highways and backroads, scraped to the sides, though it is no longer white, having taken on the color of dirt. There's a potter in Lewiston who pays one hundred dollars a truckload for the ash. He mixes it to a fine glaze that fires iridescent and makes coffee mugs, salad bowls, garlic keepers. I have several pieces, MT. ST. HELENS 1980 stamped on the bottom, reminders less of the volcano than of the general feel of that spring as a time of second chances, of new horizons forming.

I lay in my bed that night, the ash still falling, and my dreams were full of the words I was learning, the stories that filled the books, the poems whose puzzle I might yet unravel. Prompted by my English professor, I was already planning to take more literature courses, perhaps even a creative writing class. I didn't know how her encouragement would define my future, how I would rediscover that lost part of myself—that child who had spent hours at a time reading and rereading the legends of King Arthur and the trials of Robin Hood, swept away from her house in the woods by words so lovely and exotic, she repeated them for days: *Excalibur, Nottingham, crabtree staff, a flagon of rich Canary wine.* Somewhere in me, there was still that young girl, sifting the water for jewels, unearthing the pearly sarcophagi, testing the flint with her teeth, tasting the world's salty promise.

WHERE I LIVE NOW, with my husband and children in the canyon above the Clearwater, is only a few miles from those feeding streams of my childhood. During spring thaw the trees, ungrounded by the wash of high current, float past us fully rooted. Old logjams from previous floods break loose; new ones pile against the bridge footings and small islands. Each becomes a nest of lost things: fishing lures, loops of rope, men's undershirts, women's shoes, a single dowel from the rail of a crib.

I wonder, sometimes, if my own life's mementos are contained in those tangles, perhaps a barrette I lost while fishing Deer Creek, or one of my mother's pie tins that my brother and I used to pan for gold. Or the tree itself, fallen from the creek bank I sat on as a child while searching for the mussel shells we called angel wings, though they were mahogany brown and often broken.

What the river takes, the river gives, and so it is with my life here. Each hour I spend with my feet near water, I feel more deeply rooted; the farther away I get, the less sure I am of my place in the world. I have known this river from its feeding waters to its mouth where it meets the Snake. I have known it before the dam and after. I have known it as a child knows water, as a lover knows water, and now as a mother who watches her own children bend at the waist, leaning forward to bring up the pods of periwinkles, the sandy shells and broken bits of blue glass worn smooth by the current's rush and tumble.

Many afternoons I pull on my vest, gather my rod, walk into the river one step at a time. My feet slide from the shoulders of rock; my toes wedge between boulders. I am timid about this, moving out toward center, where the water is deepest, where the big fish might lie.

The Clearwater is not easy. Too wide to cast from shore, too swift, too pocked with hidden currents and sudden holes. I go at it anyway, determined to find my place of stability, the water at my belly, my thighs numbing with cold.

My husband fishes below me. On shore, our daughter and son dig pools in the sand. I watch as they flash in the sun, and it is as though I am reliving my own young life, as though I exist in two dimensions and know the pleasure of each—the child's pure delight in the moment; the woman's recognition of continuance, of the water around her, the sun on her face.

I choose a fly I think the fish might favor, its color that of the day's light and leaves and wings. I praise its tufts and feathers, its hackle and tail. I load the line, thinking not of the S I must make through air but of the place above sand where the water eddies, the V above whitecaps, the purl below stone.

I do not think of the line or the fly or the fish as much as I think about the water moving against and around me, how the sky fills my eyes and the noise that isn't noise fills my ears—the hum of just-waking or sleep, blood rush, dream rush, the darkness coming on, the air.

I forget to watch for the fish to strike, forget to note the catch, the spin, the sinking. I pull the line in, let it loop at my waist, sing it out again, and again. The trout will rise, or they won't. The nubbin of fur and thread will turn to caddis, black ant, stone fly, bee, or it will simply settle on the water and remain a human's fancy. Either way, it's magic to me, and so I stay until my feet are no longer my own but part of the river's bed. How can I move them? How can I feel my way back to shore, where my family is calling that it's time to go home? They are hungry, and the shadows have taken the canyon. They are cold.

From my place in the water, they seem distant to me. I must seem like a fool, numb to my rib cage, no fish to show. But I am here in the river, half in, half out, a wader of two worlds. I smile. I wave. I am where nothing can reach me.

IT HAS TAKEN ME TIME to understand the need I feel to be consumed by the river. I want its sound in my ears, its smell, its taste. I want to be immersed—my hands, my feet, my hips—just as I was as a child, when the preacher leaned me back into the icy waters of Reeds Creek and I felt my legs let go, floating for that moment without resistance, without air or sky or land, baptized, reborn, swept free of all sin.

Perhaps what I see in the river is some mirror of the contradictions that make up my own life—the calm surface, the turbulent pull beneath, the creation, the infinite capacity for destruction. Several times a week I drive the river road to Lewiston, where I teach at Lewis-Clark State College, where I mark the chalkboards I once took notes from, where I lead my students through the same books that jolted me into awareness. The drive takes me past Cherry Lane Bridge and its fragrant fields of alfalfa, past Myrtle, where there once was a bar famous for its fights and fast women, where my uncles, pressed into child care, had often felt the need to stop for a cold beer before logging the final miles of our trip. I remember how they came back to the Chevy, smelling of whiskey and Kools and pepperoni, suddenly happy in the company of children entrusted to them for the day.

As I drive, I see how the dark silhouette of my travel wavers across the river's shallows, grows fat, then thin, disappears altogether at the deepest curves. I think how that twin has always been with me—through my memories of childhood journeys, from the woods to town and back, always the long blue ribbon of water, the blacker thread of road, our outline weaving between sun and shade, an apparition through yellow pine and red fir, through the tight growth of paradise trees, through snake grass and the shiny, oiled leaves of ivy.

Nights, as I follow the winding highway back home, I look toward the water, casting the moon from its belly in a current of silver. Driving by water is a seduction, I think, a temptation to come and join and know. So easy, the lift off asphalt, the wind, the slow sinking. The final fear to face no fear at all but a rare, consuming sleep. There have been times in my life when such oblivion seemed more enticing than the impossible path before me. I remember those hours of limbo as though I were already drowned—everything a swirl of gray noise and no light.

I am grateful that farther up the road is my family: my daughter who still lolls into dreams with her thumb in her mouth—that small mouth falling open as I trace her lips and wonder at their delicate resistance; my son, weaned at two, whose fingers still caress my breasts when he thinks I'm not looking; my husband who waits for me, porch light on. "You're home now," he says. He takes my coat, sits me down at our table. He feeds me good bread, roasted chicken, squash from our garden baked soft and sweet. He locks the doors against the outside, pulls back the sheets and covers me. He tells me to sleep, that he is there, that he means to stay. The house murmurs its familiar sounds, my lover slides in beside me, and I smell the warm-earth smell that is his.

Is THIS WHEREIN FAITH LIES—the unlearning of old lessons, the impossible projection of love? Is it found here, in the everyday rituals of sustenance, the food on the table, the nightly kisses, the mornings all new and intimate, when we rise and greet one another, blinking in the light?

"Shadrach, Meshach, and Abed-nego, into the fire they had to go," our Sunday school once sang. "But did they burn up? Oh, no!" we exclaimed. It was faith that delivered them and faith that I clung to, desperately, because it seemed something elusive, easily lost. And if faith were lost, so was I. We might all be tested by fire, we were told, before the Lord's coming. Without adequate faith, I would be bound over like the three men and cast into Nebuchadnezzar's fire but without the protection of God's asbestos angel. I would burn forever for my sins.

What I feel now is not the faith of my childhood, but perhaps it is one that has taught me the other, the Bible and its sermons that have allowed me to recognize faith when I feel it: a letting go of control; a giving over to the forces you believe are shaping your life, whether it be God or the land or the love of a child or the look on your lover's face when he turns to you in his sleep and whispers your name.

Summer nights, when I lie with my family on the deck, the moon at our fingers, the river at our feet, I trace the meteors' fall, name the constellations. Cassiopeia, the Archer, Cygnus the Swan: for me, it was one simple star, but I want for my children a larger heaven. Still, each time, I name it first, that star they might always find themselves by—Polaris forever to the north.

From the tallest tree, an owl calls its honest question. It waits in the branches above us, somewhere between earth and sky, patient for its dinner, shedding light from its wings. I hear the sound of the river, the soft breathing of my son and daughter as they drift toward sleep. My husband reaches his hand across them, touches my face. I wonder if, at that moment, he knows how much I fear such a perfect world. For this is not a fairy tale. It is the story of a woman still struggling to understand what she is made of, all that she has been and might yet be.

———

"I KNEW IT WOULD BE HARD for you," my father says to me. "I just didn't know how hard. What I never doubted was that you would be okay. I never doubted that at all."

I wonder, sometimes, at my father's vision. I watch him as he sits in his easy chair, smoking, reading the Bible, watching TV, and I see the inner absorption, the way he is always thinking, thinking in that way that makes him deaf to the kitchen noise and the traffic and the voices of his family, calling him for dinner. He is a traveler, journeying inward, through the maze of his heart and mind and soul. Often, my father and I sit together in silence until I rise to begin the reclamation of socks and shoes and toys, preparing to take my leave; it is then that his head comes up and he begins our conversation, as though it has taken him all evening to decide what questions deserve asking, words to him like desert water, spare and necessary.

My grandmother is dead now. My mother and father have moved into her house, and I feel immersed in her memory each time I visit. It isn't perfect yet, this truce my parents and I hold between us, but I can come to their home, eat at their table, and sometimes say what matters. Often, my brother brings his wife and children. He is an engineer, a good husband and father. He is an elder in the church; he keeps the faith. His memories are not always the same as mine, and so we work toward common ground, toward those places and stories we share. As with my father, I find my strongest connection with my brother when we go back into the wilderness, when we hunt the draws and wade the river together.

My mother and I have come to our own place of repose. Her elbow rubs against mine as we wash and dry the plates and silverware, and I think how satisfied I am to work next to her. Her body is familiar, her light scent of perfume a sure comfort. Her only need, it has often seemed, is for harmony, something my father and I have, in the past, been incapable of offering. I have come to realize that the will of my beautiful mother, who demanded of herself invisibility, who struggled to suppress her desire for anything beyond the happiness of her family and the good of her faith, may have been the strongest will of all. There are times when I look at her and am struck again by the blue of her eyes: so light, almost white, she would say with regret in her voice, as though the wash of color, like a high-clouded sky, were something to be ashamed of.

All those years of warning came of love—the best she could do without a voice, without the words to articulate the fear she felt for me. I know so few of her stories, have so little sense of her life's narrative. And because she has not spoken her stories, I have, in the past, allowed myself to believe that there weren't any, that her life was an uninterrupted line leading from her childhood to marriage and the birth of her children.

Over the years it has taken me to write this, I have, in small, interlocking pieces, told my mother and father the story of David Jenkins. And because my father believes that everything works together for the good, he tells me that there is a reason why I have chosen the paths I have walked.

"It's not that I want to hear these things," he says. "But I'm glad you've told me. It helps me understand."

I think of the puzzles he worked those long winter nights

in the woods, each piece so carefully considered. "Farther along," he would sing, "we'll know all about it. Farther along, we'll understand why": more a wish than a prayer.

Yet here I am, having survived my lessons, having learned more than anyone might have foreseen. Because my father gave me both reason to rebel and the means to do it. Because he believed, even in the darkest hour, that I would find my way out.

On the curving highway below my house, my father drives each day, hauling his load of wood chips. It is a dangerous road, one he cannot take his eyes from. He raises his hand anyway, in case I am watching, and in that small, transitory gesture is an acknowledgment of connection, of faith in the air that binds us.

MY HOME IN THE WOODS is gone now. Company land, after all, worth more as commodity than domicile. The narrow house we called a shotgun shack, the shallow lawn with its river-rock barbecue, the root cellar with its bottles and old blankets—all of it scavenged, then burned to the ground.

The first time I saw it this way, having remembered it whole for so many years, I walked like a wanderer through what once had been the living room, or maybe my bedroom—so little left to orient myself by. Even the trees that had anchored the corners of the land had been cut and hauled off; smaller trees had sprung up, tipping the sky twenty feet above my head: grand fir in the laundry room; blue spruce in the kitchen.

Bits of porcelain shone through the grass like shards of bone. Every window, every pane, shattered into sharp angles, half buried in duff, a field of glass and metal and scorched cloth, a dark yawn in the hillside where my father once prayed—all that was left of my life there, that short period of time when the spring gave us water and the trees gave us shade, when my parents were poor but seemed happy, before I learned what my body might know.

I felt an overwhelming sense of loss—not just for the hollow, but for that memory of myself in its palm. Because it is no longer there, because even its ruins have been buried, it feels as though it never existed—some dream I had come to believe and now must forget.

It is in this place above the river that I set down the words I hope to live by. That woman I was before, she has no place here. Yet even as I say this, I realize I cannot separate myself from that other. She is both me and not me, just as I am both of the past and the present. If I reject what I am made of, I leave nothing to guide my own daughter except the silence that is my inheritance, nothing for my son, whose birthright is half the truth of what passes between man and woman.

I think of the Inuit way: a wolf bone whittled to a point at both ends, coiled and frozen in blubber, left along the path of bears. The bear eats it and weakens slowly, over miles, over days, the bone twisting and slashing, killing from the inside out. Shame feels this way, swallowed and sharp, working its way deeper with each move to dislodge the pain, so that finally, we lie still, dying with blood in our mouths. We eat our stories and starve.

MINE IS A STORY OF FIRE, the ravening and purging, the exhaustion of air, the cinders and flames of renewal. Mine, too, is the story of intimate waters: the womb, the runoff of spring thaw, the cold dash of baptism, the tidal flow of my seasons, the birth-glide of my children in their paraffined skins. It is the story of the wilderness I was born to and left and reentered, the prayers of my faith and its betrayal, the touch of hands both holy and damned. Deer lick and trout flash, the voices rising in hallelujahs of praise, belt lash, the salving caress, the cry of shame: I am all of it, and will always be.

From that place in the woods where the fires burned, where my father returned to us weary and watchful, his clothes smelling like coals from the furnace, I come to this bend in the river, where the water runs deep, where, in spring and fall, the last steelhead and salmon nose into stone and anchor themselves to rest. It is here that I take up my journey, chart my course by that true north star, and begin once again to believe.

ACKNOWLEDGMENTS

MY HUSBAND AND CHILDREN—Bob, Philip, Jordan, and Jace—have given endless comfort and encouragement; they have kept me anchored in the present; they have fed me when I could not feed myself.

I could not have made this journey without the love of my parents, whose willingness to travel the old roads with me has given me strength and taught me yet another lesson in the ways of the heart. The support of my brother and his family is a gift.

Thanks to others who have offered their wisdom and have shared their own stories so that I might know what good company I keep: Mary Clearman Blew, Claire Davis, Dennis Held, Robert Johnson, Lisa Norris, and Christy Thompson. Keith and Shirley Browning, Vana Vernon, Ann Jones, and Renée Wayne Golden have aided and guided me. Special thanks to Bruce Tracy, who hears the story when I cannot.

KIM BARNES'S *In the Wilderness* was awarded the PEN/Jerard Fund Award and was a finalist for the 1997 Pulitzer Prize and PEN/Martha Albrand Award. Her stories and poems have appeared in numerous journals, including *The Georgia Review* and *Shenandoah.* She lives with her husband, the poet Robert Wrigley, and their children above the Clearwater River in Idaho.